# WORKBOOK
## with Digital Pack

**3**

CEFR
**B1+**

# TH!NK

## SECOND EDITION

T0384699

**Herbert Puchta,**
**Jeff Stranks &**
**Peter Lewis-Jones**
with Clare Kennedy

CAMBRIDGE
UNIVERSITY PRESS

# ACKNOWLEDGEMENTS

**Acknowledgements**

The authors and publishers acknowledge the following sources of copyright material and are grateful for the permissions granted. While every effort has been made, it has not always been possible to identify the sources of all the material used, or to trace all copyright holders. If any omissions are brought to our notice, we will be happy to include the appropriate acknowledgements on reprinting and in the next update to the digital edition, as applicable.

**Key**: U = Unit, WU = Welcome Unit.

<u>Text</u>

**U6**: Text from *The Mind Map Level* 3 *Lower-intermediate* by David Morrison, Cambridge English: Towards FCE. Copyright © Cambridge University Press - All rights reserved; **U12**: Text from *Bullring Kid and Country Cowboy Level 4 Intermediate* by Louise Clover, Cambridge English: Towards FCE. Copyright © Cambridge University Press - All rights reserved.

<u>Photography</u>

The following photographs are sourced from Getty Images.

**WU**: FatCamera/E+; kali9/iStock/Getty Images Plus; **U1**: Westend61; NoSystem images/E+; monkeybusinessimages/iStock/Getty Images Plus; **U2**: duncan1890/ DigitalVision Vectors; Mark Coggins/Moment Open; S. Greg Panosian/E+; Paola Giannoni/E+; **U3**: jojoo64/iStock/Getty Images Plus; claudiodivizia/iStock/Getty Images Plus; GoodGnom/DigitalVision Vectors; Westend61; William Perugini/ Cultura; Christoph Hetzmannseder/Moment; **U4**: Comezora/Moment; **U5**: Jeff Greenough; Steve Granitz/WireImage; Westend61; Scott E Barbour/The Image Bank; **U6**: Joseph L. Murphy/Getty Images Sport; Antonio Lopez Martinez/EyeEm; Photography by Mangiwau/Moment; JEAN-FRANCOIS MONIER/AFP; Andre Vieira/Getty Images News; aydinmutlu/iStock/Getty Images Plus; **U7**: FatCamera/ E+; LRArmstrong/iStock/Getty Images Plus; Nick Dale/Design Pics; **U8**: Qi Yang/ Moment; Luis Diaz Devesa/Moment; tane-mahuta/iStock/Getty Images Plus; andresr/E+; Bryan Mullennix/EyeEm; **U9**: JohnnyGreig/E+; Glowimages; Naomi Rahim/Moment; Marco Simoni/Cultura; **U10**: monkeybusinessimages/iStock/ Getty Images Plus; chee gin tan/E+; JazzIRT/E+; **U11**: Martin Harvey/The Image Bank; **U12**: bymuratdeniz/E+; Bettmann; Bruce Glikas/FilmMagic; Juanmonino/E+.

Cover photography by Mustafagull/E+/Getty Images; George Pachantouris/ Moment/Getty Images.

The following photographs are sourced from other libraries/sources.

**U3**: konstantinks/Shutterstock; Arcady/Shutterstock; **U5**: Cover of *The Boy Who Biked the World: On the Road to Africa* (part 1), Nov 2011. Copyright © Eye Books. Reused with permission; **U6**: Realimage/Alamy Stock Photo; ton koene/Alamy Stock Photo; Charles O. Cecil/Alamy Stock Photo.

<u>Illustrations</u>

**WU**: Ben Scruton; **U1, U8**: Daniela Geremia; **U2**: Mark Ruffle; **U3**: Martin Sanders; Ben Scruton; **U4**: Daniela Geremia; Daniela Geremia; Ben Scruton; **U6**: Ben Scruton; Daniela Geremia; Adam Linley; Martin Sanders; **U7**: Mark Ruffle; Martin Sanders; **U10**: Adam Linley; **U12**: Ben Scruton; Daniela Geremia.

Grammar Rap video stills: Silversun Media Group.

Full video acknowledgements can be found in the online Teacher's Resources.

Audio Production: Leon Chambers.

# CONTENTS

# WELCOME

## A THAT'S ENTERTAINMENT
### *let* and *allow*

**1** **Rewrite the sentences using the words in brackets.**

House rules: what my parents let or don't let me do.

**0** My parents don't let me play loud music in my bedroom. (allowed)

*I'm not allowed to play loud music in my* _____
*bedroom.* _____

**1** My parents let me stay up late at the weekend. (allowed)

_____

**2** I'm allowed to practise my electric guitar in the garage. (let)

_____

**3** I'm not allowed to go out on school nights. (let)

_____

**4** My parents let me have parties at home. (allowed)

_____

**5** I'm not allowed to go to concerts on my own. (let)

_____

### Music

**2** **Unscramble the words and write them in the correct list. Add two more items to each list.**

inapo | jzaz | laslacsic | oilniv
opp | par | srumd | tagriu

**Musical instruments**　　**Types of music**

1 _____　　7 _____

2 _____　　8 _____

3 _____　　9 _____

4 _____　　10 _____

5 _____　　11 _____

6 _____　　12 _____

**3** **Complete the sentences so that they are true for you.**

**1** I really like listening to _____

**2** I never listen to _____

**3** I play _____

**4** I'd love to play _____

### Verbs of perception

**4** **Complete the sentences.**

feel | looks | smells | tastes

**1** I love your new haircut. It _____ fantastic!

**2** Your hands _____ very cold. Are you OK?

**3** This fruit juice _____ disgusting! I don't want any more.

**4** Lunch _____ really good. Let's eat now!

**5** **Complete the sentences with the correct form of the verbs in brackets.**

**1** Why _____ you _____ (smell) the milk? Is it bad?

**2** What's for dinner? It _____ (smell) great.

**3** What _____ you _____ (look) at?

**4** You _____ (not look) great. What's the matter?

**5** This sandwich _____ (taste) awful. What's in it?

**6** Why _____ you _____ (taste) the soup again?

**7** A Why _____ you _____ my scarf (feel)?
B I love it! It's just so soft.

**8** Leah's gone home because she _____ (not feel) well.

### The big screen

**6** **Complete the word puzzle and find the name of one of the *Avengers* films.**

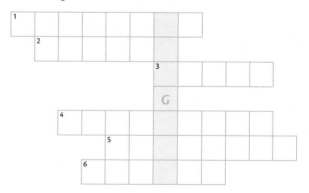

**1** a serious film with lots of exciting moments

**2** a film with a lot of explosions and car chases

**3** a serious story with realistic characters

**4** a cartoon-style film, usually for children

**5** a _____ comedy is a love story that makes you laugh, and maybe cry

**6** a film that makes you laugh

## Present perfect tenses

7 Circle the correct options.

1 I haven't *watched / been watching* TV for more than a week.
2 We've *seen / been seeing* this film before.
3 The cinema has *shown / been showing* the same film for weeks now.
4 If you've *lost / been losing* your ticket, you can't come in.
5 They've *waited / been waiting* in the cinema queue for three hours.
6 You've *read / been playing* that game for an hour. Can I have a go now?

## TV programmes

8 Match the parts to make types of TV programme.

0 chat — com
1 game — programme
2 drama — show
3 sit — news
4 sports — show
5 the — series

## SUMMING UP

9 Complete the dialogue with the words and phrases in the list. There are three you don't need.

> 're watching | let | 've been watching
> the news | jazz | allowed to | watch
> to watch | watched | 've watched
> guitar | drama series

**Logan** Max, it's my turn ¹_____ TV.

**Max** Just give me 20 more minutes.

**Logan** But you ²_____ TV for more than two hours now. You're not even ³_____ watch so much TV. Does Mum know?

**Max** Yes, she does. Anyway, I'm almost finished.

**Logan** Yes but I want to watch ⁴_____ and it starts in five minutes.

**Max** You can ⁵_____ it later. I really need to see the end of this.

**Logan** What is it that you ⁶_____, anyway?

**Max** *Crime Wave.*

**Logan** What, the American ⁷_____?

**Max** Yes, that's right. This is the last episode in the series. I can't miss it. I ⁸_____ all the others. I want to know how it ends.

**Logan** I'll tell you how it ends. The police officer is the murderer. Now ⁹_____ me watch my show.

## B TIME TO ACT
## Our endangered planet

1 🔊 W.01 Complete the sentences with the words in the list. Then listen and check.

> climate change | flooding | fumes
> litter | pollution | smog

1 With the Earth's temperature rising each year, many scientists now believe _____ is the biggest threat to our planet.
2 _____ from factories and cars are creating huge _____ problems and many of the world's largest cities are permanently covered by thick _____.
3 There has been serious _____ across the area and many people have had to leave their homes.
4 I get so angry when I see people dropping _____ in the streets. Why can't they use the bins?

## Question tags

2 Match the sentences with the question tags.

1 You don't care about the environment, ☐
2 Helen campaigns for the environment, ☐
3 Global warming is getting serious, ☐
4 The world isn't going to end tomorrow, ☐
5 Your friends didn't go on the protest march, ☐
6 Mark threw the rubbish in the bin, ☐
7 The Earth can't take much more, ☐
8 Science can find a solution, ☐

a isn't it?  e didn't he?
b did they?  f do you?
c can it?  g is it?
d can't it?  h doesn't she?

3 Complete the sentences with question tags.

1 You're from Argentina, _____?
2 This is pretty easy, _____?
3 You know him, _____?
4 They played really well, _____?
5 Qi and Bo don't speak English, _____?
6 She's working in London now, _____?
7 He can't sing, _____?
8 Tom won't be late, _____?
9 You've been to Canada, _____?
10 I shouldn't have said that, _____?

## Party time

**4** **Match the parts of the sentences.**

Am I ready for the party? Well, so far …

1 I haven't found anywhere ☐
2 I haven't got permission ☐
3 I haven't drawn up ☐
4 So clearly I haven't sent out ☐
5 I haven't hired ☐
6 Or even got the money to pay ☐
7 I haven't decorated ☐
8 And I haven't organised ☐

a the guest list.
b the food.
c a DJ.
d the deposit for one.
e the room.
f from Mum and Dad.
g to have the party.
h any invitations.

## Indefinite pronouns

**5** **Complete the sentences with the words in the list.**

> anyone | everyone | everything
> no one | nothing | nowhere
> something | somewhere

The party was terrible.

1 I didn't know _____ .
2 _____ I tried to speak to just ignored me.
3 There was _____ to eat at all.
4 You had to pay for your drinks and _____ on the list was really expensive.
5 We wanted to leave our coats _____ but there was no cloakroom.
6 It was so crowded, there was _____ to sit.
7 Sally wanted _____ to do so we went to the dance floor.
8 But _____ was dancing. We were the only ones!

## Arranging a party

**6** **Complete the dialogue with the words in the list. There are two you don't need.**

> anyone | anything | decorating
> everyone | everything | everywhere
> get | hiring | nowhere | organising
> sent out | something

Sonya  So, Rory, is ¹_____ ready for the party tomorrow?

Rory   I think so. I've just finished ²_____ the room and ³_____ the food.

Sonya  So there will be ⁴_____ to eat?

Rory   Yes, and to drink.

Sonya  So who's coming? ⁵_____ I know?

Rory   There'll be loads of people you know. I ⁶_____ about 30 invitations.

Sonya  That's a lot of people. Did you have to ⁷_____ permission from your parents?

Rory   Of course, I'm having the party at our house.

Sonya  Is there ⁸_____ I can do?

Rory   Well, you could bring some music with you. I'm not ⁹_____ a DJ.

Sonya  OK, I'll bring some music that will get ¹⁰_____ dancing.

## SUMMING UP

**7**  🔊 W.02   **Put the dialogue in order. Listen and check.**

☐ Rob  Of course there is. I'm organising a protest march for Sunday. Do you want to join me?

☐ Rob  That's a shame. But you could donate a bit of money, couldn't you?

☐ Rob  Yes, and I don't think the government will do anything about it.

☐ Rob  So that is why I think we should do something about it.

1 Rob  I think the pollution in our city is getting worse each year.

☐ Mia  I'm afraid I left my wallet at home. Sorry.

☐ Mia  So do I. It's a real problem, isn't it?

☐ Mia  Neither do I. They never do.

☐ Mia  But there's nothing we can do, is there?

☐ Mia  I'd love to but I can't. I'm busy.

# C IN MY OPINION, …
## Feeling under the weather

**1  Match the parts of the sentences.**

1  Take this medicine and you'll feel
2  I always get
3  Dad's going to hospital to have
4  Can you phone the doctor and make
5  Why don't you see
6  You need to take more

a  sick when I travel by car.
b  an appointment for me?
c  a doctor about your headaches?
d  exercise to lose some weight.
e  better in half an hour.
f  an operation next week.

**2  Complete the sentences with the correct form of the phrases in the list.**

> take some exercise | feel sick | have an operation
> make an appointment | get better | see a doctor

1  I hope you _____ soon.

4  Hello, I'd like to _____ with Dr Hill.

2  He's _____ .

5  I think you need to _____ .

3  That cat needs to _____ .

6  I _____ !

## Giving advice

**3  Complete each piece of advice with one word.**

*I get really tired when I have to run.*

1  You _____ take more exercise.
2  You _____ better see a doctor.
3  You _____ to lose some weight.
4  You should _____ eat so much.
5  You had _____ be careful.
6  You ought _____ join a gym.

**4  Write one piece of advice for each of these people.**

1  'I can't do my homework.'

_____

2  'I'm bored.'

_____

3  'I haven't got any money.'

_____

4  'I'm new at school and I don't know anyone.'

_____

## Comparisons

**5** **Complete the sentences with the words in brackets and any other necessary words.**

1 The Oscars are _____ (important) award ceremony in the film industry.

2 The host wasn't _____ (funny) the guy who did it last year.

3 The ceremony was a lot _____ (long).

4 The best actor's speech was _____ (bad) I can remember.

5 However, I think the actors were dressed _____ (beautiful) than usual.

6 Apparently one actress was wearing _____ (expensive) dress in the world.

**6** **Rewrite the sentences so that they mean the same thing.**

1 It's hotter today than it was yesterday.
Yesterday wasn't _____

2 I've never seen a more boring film in my life.
That was _____

3 She's the kindest person I know.
I don't know anyone as _____

4 I used to remember things more easily when I was younger.
I don't _____

5 Martin and Simon play tennis equally as well.
Simon plays tennis _____

6 It's the most expensive car in the world.
There isn't a car as _____

## SUMMING UP

**7** (◁) **W.03** **Put the dialogue in order. Listen and check.**

☐ **Brody** I'm going to. I've made an appointment.

☐ **Brody** I'm not sure. Every day I wake up more tired than the day before.

☐ **Brody** I know. I'm not sure I can wait that long.

☐1 **Brody** I've been feeling really sick recently.

☐ **Brody** The problem is the appointment's for next Thursday. They didn't have one any earlier.

☐ **Verity** Oh dear. What's wrong?

☐ **Verity** You'd better call them and tell them it's an emergency.

☐ **Verity** What! That's a week from now.

☐ **Verity** Sick and tired. You should see a doctor.

☐ **Verity** Well, hopefully, he'll be able to help you get better.

## D HELP!
### Reported speech

**1** **Report the conversation.**

0 **Amy** I need help.

1 **Jen** What's the matter?

2 **Amy** I can't find my key.

3 **Jen** Check inside your pocket.

4 **Amy** I've already done that.

5 **Jen** Have you checked the door?

6 **Amy** Why do you want me to do that?

7 **Jen** That's where you always leave them.

0 Amy said that _____*she needed help.*_____

1 Jen asked Amy _____

2 Amy said that _____

3 Jen told Amy _____

4 Amy said _____

5 Jen asked Amy _____

6 Amy asked Jen _____

7 Jen said _____

## Sequencing words

**2** **Unscramble the sequencing words.**

1 rafte _____

2 hent _____

3 yanllif _____

4 ta rifts _____

**3** **Complete the story with words from Exercise 2.**

1 _____ we thought we'd never get out. The door just wouldn't open.

2 _____ five minutes of kicking the door, we were exhausted.

3 _____ Dad found the key in his pocket.

4 _____ we got the door open.

## Asking for and offering help

**4** **Complete the words.**

1 Have you got a f_____ m_____ ?

2 C_____ I help you?

3 Can you l_____ me a h_____ ?

4 Could you h_____ me with something?

5 Do you n_____ any help?

**5 Put the dialogue in order.**

☐ Mimi I said that I was going to tidy it after I'd done my homework.

☐ Mimi What deal?

☐ Mimi Could you help me with my homework?

☐ Mimi That's the same deal we had before!

☐ Mimi But you said you'd help me.

☐ Mimi Dad, have you got a few minutes?

☐ Dad Tidy your room and then I'll lend you a hand with your homework.

☐ Dad And you said you'd tidy your room – remember?

☐ Dad That depends. What do you want?

☐ Dad I'm sorry, but I'm a bit busy.

☐ Dad So, I'll make you a deal.

## IT vocabulary

**6 Match the parts of the sentences.**

1 Have you seen that Matt has posted ☐

2 Before you start you have to key ☐

3 I'm having a problem installing ☐

4 Send me the photo – you can attach ☐

5 I'm going to upload ☐

6 I'm sorry – I deleted your ☐

7 I'm not sure how to activate ☐

8 It's taking ages to download ☐

a all my holiday photos online.

b message. Can you send it again?

c flight mode on this tablet.

d this program. Can you help?

e this file. It's really big.

f another photo on the school website?

g it to an email.

h in your password.

## Passive tenses

**7 Rewrite the sentences in the passive.**

1 Five people have posted new messages on my website.

Five new messages _____

_____

2 Someone uploaded the video onto YouTube.

The video _____

_____

3 Someone had already keyed in my password.

My password _____

_____

4 Two million people have downloaded this video.

This video _____

_____

5 The teacher sent the email to all the students.

All the students _____

_____

6 The program is attaching the file to the message.

The file _____

_____

## SUMMING UP

**8 Complete the dialogue with words and phrases in the list.**

> files | said I | buy | has accessed
> said he | passwords | has been
> delete | installed | is being | then

Loris My computer [1]_____ hacked.

Anne What do you mean, 'hacked'?

Loris Someone [2]_____ my computer from another computer.

Anne Really? How do you know?

Loris A program has been [3]_____ that has deleted loads of my [4]_____ .

Anne That's terrible.

Loris And all my [5]_____ have been stolen, too.

Anne So what are you going to do?

Loris My computer [6]_____ looked at by an expert at the moment. He [7]_____ could hopefully [8]_____ the program.

Anne And if he can't?

Loris He [9]_____'d have to buy a new computer.

Anne Well, if you do, remember to [10]_____ better anti-virus software.

Loris Yes, and [11]_____ create some new passwords!

# 1 BIG DECISIONS

Grammar rap!
▶ 02

## Ⓖ GRAMMAR
### Present tenses (review) → SB p.14

**1** ★☆☆ **For each sentence, choose the correct tense. Write PS (present simple), PC (present continuous), PPS (present perfect simple) or PPC (present perfect continuous).**

0   I <u>haven't decided</u> what I want to do yet. __PPS__

1   I always <u>do</u> my homework when I get home from school. _____

2   Liam <u>hasn't been doing</u> well at school for a few months. _____

3   My sister<u>'s always talking</u> on her phone. _____

4   They<u>'ve been thinking</u> about buying a new house for more than a year now. _____

5   Lewis <u>has forgotten</u> to do his homework again. _____

6   Stella <u>doesn't want</u> to go to university next year. _____

7   It's the last week of term, so we <u>aren't doing</u> very much at school. _____

**2** ★★☆ **Complete the sentences with the words in the list.**

> 've been writing | don't write | 've played
> 's playing | hasn't been playing | plays
> haven't written | 'm writing

1   No, he isn't busy. He _____ a game on the computer.

2   I _____ my party invitations. Who should I invite?

3   Most people _____ letters any more, just emails.

4   I _____ all morning. My hand's tired.

5   My cousin usually _____ tennis twice a day. He loves it.

6   I _____ to thank my aunt for my present yet. I must do it tonight.

7   We _____ all of these games. Have you got any others?

8   Celia isn't very good at the piano. She _____ for very long.

**3** ★★☆ (Circle) **the correct options.**

We [1]*do / 're doing* some really important exams at school over the next few weeks, so I [2]*spend / 'm spending* most of my free time studying for them at the moment. Normally, the two things I [3]*like / 'm liking* most in life are TV and computer games, but I [4]*don't watch / 'm not watching* any TV and I [5]*don't play / 'm not playing* computer games while I've got exams. I usually [6]*help / am helping* my dad in his shop at the weekends. He [7]*doesn't pay / isn't paying* me a lot, but I [8]*like / 'm liking* getting the money. I [9]*don't work / 'm not working* for a while, though. I [10]*need / 'm needing* the time for revision.

**4** ★★☆ **Complete the dialogues. Use the present perfect simple or continuous.**

1   **A** You look tired, Paula.
    **B** I am. I _____ very well lately. (not sleep)

2   **A** _____ your homework? (finish)
    **B** Nearly.

3   **A** Where's Eddie?
    **B** I don't know. I _____ him for a few hours. (not see)

4   **A** You're dirty. What _____ ? (do)
    **B** Helping Mum in the garden.

**5** ★★★ **Complete the dialogue with the verbs in brackets. Use the present simple, present continuous, present perfect simple or present perfect continuous.**

**Jules**   [0] __*Have*__ you __*seen*__ (see) Elena recently? I [1]_____ (not see) her for weeks.

**Dylan**   No, but she [2]_____ (text) me most days.

**Jules**   So what [3]_____ (she/do) these days?

**Dylan**   Well, she [4]_____ (train) really hard for the past month.

**Jules**   Training? For what?

**Dylan**   She [5]_____ (want) to be a professional footballer. Chelsea Football Club [6]_____ (invite) her to train with them. She starts with them on Monday.

## Future tenses (review)    → SB p.15

**6** ★★☆ Look at Greta's diary and write sentences about her plans for next week. Use the present continuous.

| **DIARY** | |
|---|---|
| **Monday** | **am:** fly to Madrid |
| | **pm:** have meeting with Pablo |
| **Tuesday** | **am:** take train to Barcelona |
| | **pm:** watch football match at Camp Nou stadium |
| **Wednesday** | **am:** fly back to London |

0  On Monday morning,  _she's flying to Madrid_  .

1  On Monday afternoon, _____ .

2  On Tuesday morning, _____ .

3  On Tuesday afternoon, _____ .

4  On Wednesday morning, _____ .

**7** ★★☆ Complete the sentences. Use a verb from the list and the correct form of *going to*. Then match the sentences with the pictures.

> make | move | not ski
> not visit | see | study

0  We____*'re going to see*____ a play tonight. I've got the tickets.

1  The car's broken down. We _____ Grandma today.

2  I _____ a curry tonight. I've just bought all the ingredients.

3  Fiona _____ Maths at Bristol University in September.

4  Penny has hurt her leg. She _____ today.

5  They're selling their house. They _____ to London.

 A  0
 B
 C
 D
 E
 F

**8** ★★☆ Read the sentences. Mark them P (prediction), I (intention), or A (arrangement).

0  I've got a tennis lesson at ten o'clock.  [A]

1  I phoned the dentist and made an appointment to see him this afternoon.  ☐

2  People living on the moon one day? Yes, definitely.  ☐

3  We've decided where to stay in London – the Ritz hotel.  ☐

4  I've decided what to do next year – travel around the world.  ☐

5  My mum, let me go to the party? No way!  ☐

**9** ★★★ Rewrite the sentences in Exercise 8 using the correct future tense.

0  *I'm playing tennis at ten o'clock.* _____

1  _____

2  _____

3  _____

4  _____

5  _____

**10** ★★★ What do you think your life will be like when you are 30?

1  (work as a)

_____

2  (have children)

_____

3  (live in a different country)

_____

## GET IT RIGHT!

### *will* vs. present continuous

**Learners often use *will* + infinitive where the present continuous is needed.**

✓ **I'm seeing** the dentist because my tooth is hurting.

✗ I'll see the dentist because my tooth is hurting.

✓ I'm not sure **we'll get** it done in time.

✗ I'm not sure we're getting it done in time.

**Complete the sentences with the correct form of a verb from the list.**

> come | go | have (x2) | not go | see | win

0  It's good that you _*are coming*_ to see me in Brazil!

1  We _____ a party next weekend – do you want to come?

2  I think Real Madrid _____ tonight.

3  My brother _____ to university next week. He's packing at the moment.

4  I _____ to Nina's party later because I have to study for tomorrow's exam.

5  We think you _____ a great time on holiday.

6  Maybe I _____ you there.

## VOCABULARY
### Making changes
→ SB p.14

**1** ★☆☆ **Match the parts of the sentences.**

1 I've decided not to make ☐
2 Noemi's trying to give ☐
3 Jason's on a diet and doing ☐
4 I'm trying to get fitter, but I'm struggling ☐
5 We needed a new hobby, so we've taken ☐
6 You must take this chance ☐
7 It's good for kids to get into ☐
8 My dad needs to eat better, but he's never going to change ☐

a really well. He's lost 5 kg already.
b with getting myself to the gym every day.
c the habit of doing some exercise every day.
d his ways.
e up photography.
f up eating chocolate, but she's finding it really difficult.
g any New Year's resolutions this year.
h to study in Australia! It won't happen again!

**2** ★★★ **Write down examples that are true for you.**

1 A resolution you'd like to make for next year:
_____

2 Something you'd like to give up:
_____

3 A school subject you do well in:
_____

4 A school subject you struggle with:
_____

5 A new hobby you'd like to take up:
_____

6 A good habit you should get into:
_____

### Life plans
→ SB p.17

**3** ★★☆ **Read the definitions and complete the phrases.**

1 t_____ t_____ w_____ : go out and see other countries
2 g_____ p_____ : be given a better job (usually in the same company)
3 l_____ s_____ : finish compulsory education
4 r_____ : finish your professional life
5 g_____ a d_____ : graduate from university
6 s_____ d_____ : have a steady job, buy a house with a partner, etc.
7 s_____ a f_____ : have children
8 s_____ a c_____ : begin your professional life

**4** ★★☆ **Complete the sentences with phrases from Exercise 3.**

1 My brother just loves being free. I can't see him ever wanting to _____ .
2 It isn't easy to _____ a new _____ when you're 50.
3 The government wants to raise the age that you can _____ to 18.
4 We certainly want to _____ one day. We'd like at least three children.
5 Katy wants to take a few years off work and _____ . She'd love to spend some time in Asia.
6 These days, many people can't afford to _____ before they're 70.
7 George _____ from university, but he's never really used it in his professional life.
8 If you work hard, you might _____ to junior manager next year.

### WordWise: Phrases with *up*
→ SB p.17

**5** ★★☆ **Put the sentences in the correct order.**

☐ Lisa  Hi, Andy. What are you <u>up to</u>?
☐ Lisa  So, what's the problem?
☐ Lisa  Is the game <u>almost up</u>?
☐ Lisa  But you love video games. So, <u>what's up</u>?
☐ Andy  I'm playing a new video game with my dad – unfortunately.
☐ Andy  No, but it isn't <u>up to me</u>. Dad wants to finish it all.
☐ Andy  Well, he isn't very good, so he can't pass the difficult levels – he just isn't <u>up to it</u>.
☐ Andy  We've been playing for hours and I want to go out.

**6** ★★☆ **Match the <u>underlined</u> phrases in Exercise 5 with their meanings.**

1 doing _____
2 capable of _____
3 nearly finished _____
4 what's the matter _____
5 my decision/choice _____

> **PRONUNCIATION**
> Linking words with *up*  Go to page 118. 🎧

# REFERENCE

## MAKING CHANGES

change your ways

do well

get into the habit (of doing something)

give (something) up

make a resolution

struggle with (something)

take (something) up

take a/the chance (to do something)

## LIFE PLANS

| | |
|---|---|
| get a degree | start a career |
| get promoted | start a family |
| leave school | settle down |
| retire | travel the world |

## PHRASES WITH *UP*

up to (an hour, etc.)

It can take **up to** 8 weeks to get a new passport.

be up to something

What **are** you and your friends **up to** on Saturday?

What's up?

**What's up**, Simon? Are you OK?

**up**

(time) is up

Stop! The time**'s up**. Stop writing and give me your test papers.

be up to somebody

If you don't enjoy your job, it**'s up to you** to find a new one.

be up to something

I'd like to invite Lucy onto the project, but I'm not sure she**'s up to it**.

# VOCABULARY *EXTRA*

1    **Match the phrases (1–6) with the definitions (a–f).**

1  get rid of
2  jump into
3  let something go
4  make a decision
5  put an end to
6  take charge of

a  decide
b  move suddenly and quickly
c  make something finish
d  throw away
e  take control
f  stop holding something

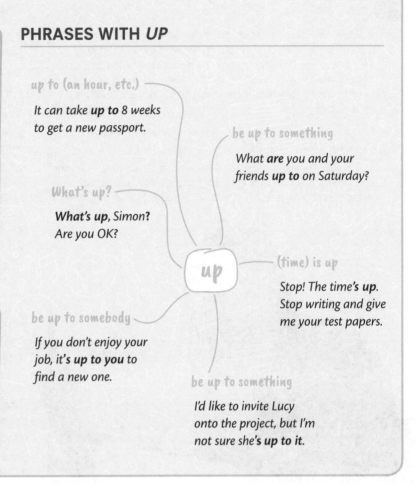

2    **Complete the sentences with the correct verb.**

1  It isn't easy to _____ a decision about your future career.
2  Little Maisie _____ go of the balloon and it flew up into the sky.
3  When the teacher arrived, he _____ an end to the game.
4  It was late, so we _____ into the car and drove off.
5  Sally's decided to _____ rid of her old clothes.
6  George _____ charge of organising the trip.

3    **Answer the questions so that they are true for you.**

1  How do you get rid of your old clothes and toys?

_____

2  What sort of decisions are the most difficult for you to make?

_____

3  If we want to make the world a better place, what things must we put an end to?

_____

# SMART GOALS

It's that time of the year again that we all look forward to so much. Exams! I'm joking, of course! Well, this year I'm not afraid because I'm going to change my ways: I'm going to use SMART goals to make sure I do well. I read an article about SMART goals. They're what all successful people in life use, apparently.

So what are SMART goals exactly and how are they going to change my life (hopefully)?

Well SMART goals are Specific, Measurable, Attainable, Relevant and Timely. See how they get their names? No? Look at the first letter of each of the words. That's what you call an acronym.

**SPECIFIC** – because they are detailed. It isn't good enough to simply say, 'I'm going to revise for my exams.' That plan's too general. A specific goal is something like: 'I'm going to spend at least 20 hours revising for each subject and make a timetable to show exactly how I'm going to do this.' That is a 'Specific' goal.

**MEASURABLE** – because you should be able to measure your goals and ask yourself questions like: 'How much have I done?'; 'How much have I still got to do?'; 'How much time do I still need?'; 'Is this nightmare ever going to end?' Well, maybe the last one isn't such a great example, but you get the idea!

**ATTAINABLE** – because your goal should be something that you can actually do. If your goal is, for example, to raise £1 million for charity, write a novel, climb Mount Everest and revise for your exams, then you might want to ask yourself if you really can do all this. Maybe you should get rid of one or two of them.

**RELEVANT** – because all your plans should help you work towards your final goal. So, for example, a plan to help your mum and dad with all the cooking, washing-up and helping out with housework might make you the most popular child in your house, but it isn't really going to help you with the revision, is it?

**TIMELY** – Your goal must have a time frame. In other words, it must have a start and a finish. There isn't much point if you're planning to finish revising a couple of weeks after your exams are over. That really doesn't make much sense.

Likewise, you need to think about when would be a good time to start. And, as they say, there's no time like the present, so I guess it might be a good idea to stop writing about SMART goals and start getting into the habit of using them!

## READING

**1** **Read the blog. How do SMART goals get their name?**

_____

**2** **Read the blog again. Mark the sentences T (true) or F (false). Then correct the false sentences.**

1 The writer enjoys doing exams. ☐

2 SMART is an example of an acronym. ☐

3 SMART goals encourage people to do more than they can. ☐

4 You don't need to think about when to start your SMART goals. ☐

**3** **Read the goal. Then follow the instructions.**

'My goal this year is to be healthier.'

1 Make this goal more specific.

2 Write down what you can measure about this goal.

3 Write an example of an attainable plan and an unattainable plan for it.

4 Write an example of a relevant and an irrelevant plan for it.

5 Make a time frame for the plan.

**4** CRITICAL THINKING **For each adjective in the acronym SMART, the writer gives an example of how a goal is not SMART and how a goal is SMART. Read the blog again and complete the table.**

| Goals | Not SMART | SMART |
|---|---|---|
| 1 Specific | | |
| 2 Measurable | | |
| 3 Attainable | | |
| 4 Relevant | | |
| 5 Timely | | |

**5** **Think of a goal you have and write a short paragraph about it. Is it a SMART goal?**

# DEVELOPING ⟩ *Writing*

## An email about a problem

**1** **INPUT** **Read the email and answer the questions.**

Who is …
1 Connor? _____
2 Damon? _____
3 Josh? _____

**2** **ANALYSE** **Read the email again and answer the questions.**

1 What specific problems does Josh have with Connor?

_____

_____

2 Underline the expressions that show you he isn't happy with these things.

_____

_____

3 What plans has he made to resolve the situation?

_____

_____

**3** (Circle) the language which introduces each of Connor's plans.

**4** **Match the content (A–D) with the paragraphs (1–4).**

A Josh describes the problem. ☐

B He says what he'll do if his plan isn't successful. ☐

C He explains his plan. ☐

D He says why he hasn't written recently. ☐

Josh
joshyB@thinkemail.com

Hi Damon,

**1** Sorry for not writing back sooner, but I've been pretty busy with school and basketball. Next week, we're in the championship final – very exciting! Here's a photo of us at basketball training last week.

**2** I've been having a few problems at school recently with a new kid called Connor. The teacher asked me to look out for him and I was happy to do that. The problem is that he's now decided I'm his best friend. He's always sending me messages and wanting to hang out with me. He's nice enough, but I'm getting a bit tired of him following me everywhere. He also gets really jealous of my friends and says some really mean things about them. That really annoys me.

**3** I know it isn't easy changing school and getting to know new people, so I'm going to help him – and I hope it'll help me, too! Next week, I'm having a welcome party for him so that he can meet some other people and make friends. I've also told him about the youth club and I think he's going to join it. The best thing is that I can't go to youth club for the next few weeks because of basketball training, so he'll have to get to know some other people.

**4** That's my plan and if it doesn't work, I'll find him some friends myself! I'll write and let you know how it goes.

See you,

Josh

**5** **PLAN** **Think of a person, real or imaginary. Write down three complaints about him / her and think of two ways to resolve the problem.**

| The problem | The solution |
| --- | --- |
| 1 He's / She's always … | |
| 2 The problem is … | |
| 3 I'm not happy with … | |

 ✓ CHECKLIST

Introduction
Describe the problem(s)
Explain your ideas for solutions
Say goodbye
Use informal language

**6** **PRODUCE** **Write an email to a friend explaining your problems and what you're going to do about them (250 words). Use your plan from Exercise 5. Make sure you include all the points in the checklist.**

## LISTENING

**1** 🔊 1.03 **Listen to three dialogues and complete the sentences.**

1 Laura and Jodie are doing _____ .

2 Jodie can't help with it because

_____ .

3 Laura's never _____ again.

4 Maddie asks Shaun about _____ .

5 Shaun feels _____ .

6 Lily wants to speak to her dad about

_____ .

7 The new teacher always _____ .

8 Lily's going to join _____ .

**2** 🔊 1.03 **Listen again and complete the dialogues.**

1 **Laura** She's ¹_____ things like this.

**Charlie** She needs to ²_____ . Next time why don't you …?

2 **Maddie** Where have you ³_____ ?

**Shaun** Er, nowhere. Well, er, you know how it is. I ⁴_____ really hard at school.

**Maddie** ⁵_____ ! You've got to relax sometimes.

**Shaun** Well, ⁶_____ Maddie, I do.

3 **Dad** Now ⁷_____ it, I haven't heard you playing much recently.

**Lily** The ⁸_____ , I'm not happy with the new teacher.

## DIALOGUE

**3** **Put the lines in order to make three short dialogues. Write them in the correct spaces.**

1 Making arrangements

A *Are you doing anything after school, Tina?*

B _____

A _____

B _____

2 Talking about future intentions

C *When do you leave school, Wang?*

D _____

C _____

D _____

3 Making personal predictions

E *Do you think you'll have children one day?*

F _____

E _____

F _____

1 I'm going to study medicine at Cambridge University.

2 One or two.

3 Probably. I hope so.

4 I'd love to, thanks.

5 Toby and I are going swimming. Do you want to come?

6 Next year in July.

7 How many do you think you'll have?

8 And what are you going to do next?

9 No, I've got nothing planned.

## PHRASES FOR FLUENCY → SB p.18

**4** **Put the words in order to make phrases.**

0 silly / be / don't  *Don't be silly* .

1 go / we / here _____ .

2 you're / star / a _____ .

3 hiding / have / been / where / you _____ ?

4 start / where / I / shall _____ ?

5 mention / you / now / it … _____ ,

**5** **Complete the dialogues with phrases in Exercise 4.**

0 **A** Shall we invite Nathan to the game with us?

**B** _____ *Don't be silly* _____ . He doesn't like football.

1 **A** You look busy. Have you got a lot to do?

**B** Busy? _____ I've got exams all week, I've got to organise Susanna's birthday, buy her a present …

2 **A** Can I make you something to eat?

**B** Thanks. I'm starving. _____ , Julio.

3 **A** I haven't seen you for weeks, Philip.

_____

**B** Nowhere. I've just been really busy.

4 **A** I know you've got to study for your exams, but would you like to come for a quick bike ride?

**B** Well, I am busy but _____ , it might be a good idea to get out for a while.

5 **A** Boys, get in here, you're 10 minutes late!

**B** _____ . We're in trouble now.

# TOWARDS B2 First for Schools

## EXAM GUIDE

**You will read a short text with eight gaps in it. For each gap, you have to choose one of four options. This part tests your knowledge of vocabulary, including phrasal verbs, collocations and the difference between words with similar meanings.**

- Read through the text quickly to get a general understanding.
- Look at the instructions and the example to make sure you understand exactly what you have to do.
- Start with gap 1. Re-read the whole sentence and pay particular attention to the words that come just *before* and *after* the gap, because they can help you choose the correct word.
- Look carefully at options A, B, C and D. Eliminate any that you are sure are wrong and focus on the others.
- For words with similar meanings, it may help to think about the context of the text to choose the right one.

For phrasal verbs, you will have one of the words and will have to choose the other.

For collocations and idioms, you may have to think about the word that sounds best.

For some gaps, you have to use your knowledge of grammar to make the right choice.

**1**  **For questions 1–2, read the text below and decide which answer (A, B, C or D) best fits each gap. There is an example at the beginning (0).**

TEENAGE RESOLUTIONS

According to a recent survey, more than 75% of 16-year-olds ⁰ __A__ at least one resolution at the beginning of each New Year. The most popular ones are ¹ _____ better at school and being nicer to family members. Other common resolutions include spending less time watching TV and giving ² _____ playing computer games altogether.

| 0 Ⓐ make | B do | C form | D find |
|---|---|---|---|
| 1 A studying | B making | C revising | D doing |
| 2 A in | B over | C out | D up |

**2**  **For questions 1–8, read the text below and decide which answer (A, B, C or D) best fits each gap. There is an example at the beginning (0).**

DECISIONS

Although I'm in my final year at school, I still haven't ⁰ __A__ what to do next. Everyone else in my family has gone to university, so I think my parents ¹ _____ me to go, too. Of course, it's up to me to decide, but the ² _____ is, I'm not sure what to study.

What's more, when my parents were young, they didn't have to pay anything to get a ³ _____ . Whereas university is going to ⁴ _____ me up to £40,000 for the course and living away from home for three years. This means I need to be absolutely certain about the course before I start. Starting a course and then ⁵ _____ it up would be a waste of time and money.

If I'm ⁶ _____ , I'd like to take a few years out to do some work and maybe ⁷ _____ the world. Perhaps with a little more life experience, I'll be able to make a better decision before I have to start my ⁸ _____ .

| 0 Ⓐ decided | B thought | C settled | D fixed |
|---|---|---|---|
| 1 A expect | B hope | C accept | D wait |
| 2 A matter | B question | C problem | D decision |
| 3 A examination | B degree | C grade | D career |
| 4 A spend | B pay | C cost | D save |
| 5 A making | B being | C doing | D giving |
| 6 A reliable | B certain | C true | D honest |
| 7 A travel | B tour | C move | D discover |
| 8 A work | B career | C progress | D activity |

# 2 A HARD LIFE

Grammar rap!

## GRAMMAR
### Narrative tenses (review) → SB p.22

**1** ★☆☆ (Circle) the correct options.

1 Joey *was / had been* tired because he *had run / had been running*.
2 My mum *was / was being* angry because I *was watching / had been watching* TV all afternoon.
3 My friends *played / had been playing* football for hours when I *arrived / was arriving*.
4 We *had been waiting / were waiting* for the concert to start for half an hour, when they *made / were making* the announcement.
5 My sister *was learning / had been learning* French for six years before she *went / was going* to France.
6 They *swam / had been swimming* for about an hour when it *started / had started* to rain.

**2** ★★☆ Complete the sentences. Use the past simple and the past continuous once in each sentence.

0 While Amelia Earhart _____*was working*_____ (work) one day, Captain Railey _____*asked*_____ (ask) her to fly to the UK from the US.
1 It _____ (sail) across the Atlantic Ocean when it _____ (hit) an iceberg.
2 People _____ (dance) in the streets after they _____ (hear) he was finally free.
3 The world _____ (watch) on TV when Neil Armstrong _____ (step) onto the moon.
4 A science student _____ (make) a medicine when he _____ (see) a new colour.
5 A plane _____ (crash) while it _____ (take off) from LaGuardia airport in New York. All the passengers survived thanks to the pilot's skill.
6 A group of young boys _____ (become) trapped while they _____ (explore) a cave. They were all rescued.

**3** ★★☆ Match the sentences in Exercise 2 with the events in world history (A–G).

- ☐ A the Hudson River air accident (2009)
- ☐ B first person on the moon (1969)
- ☐ C freedom for Nelson Mandela (1990)
- ☐ D Thai cave rescue (2018)
- ☐ E sinking of the *Titanic* (1912)
- 0 F the first woman to fly across the Atlantic (1928)
- ☐ G the discovery of purple (1856)

**4** ★★☆ Complete the sentences. Use the past perfect and the past simple once in each sentence.

Yesterday afternoon I had a guitar lesson.

0 When I _____*had finished*_____ (finish) my guitar lesson, I _____*walked*_____ (walk) home.
1 We _____ (have) dinner after I _____ (arrive) home.
2 I _____ (do) the washing-up after we _____ (eat) dinner.
3 When I _____ (finish) the washing-up, I _____ (call) my friend Tina.
4 I _____ (do) my homework after I _____ (speak) to Tina.
5 When I _____ (finish) my homework, I _____ (watch) a film.

**5** ★★★ What did you do yesterday? Write similar sentences to the ones in Exercise 4 using the past perfect and the past simple.

1 Yesterday afternoon I _____
_____
2 When _____
_____
3 _____
_____
4 _____
_____
5 _____
_____

## *would* and *used to*

→ SB p.25

6 ★☆☆ **Complete the sentences with the verbs in the list.**

be (x2) | have | have to
make | play | take

Life in the 1960s was very different from now …

1 There used to _____ public telephones in the streets.

2 Children used to _____ outside in the streets with their friends.

3 Cars didn't use to _____ seat belts.

4 TV didn't use to _____ in colour, only in black and white.

5 People didn't use to _____ many photos, just on special occasions.

6 Parents used to _____ a lot of their children's clothes.

7 You used to _____ go to a cinema to see a film.

7 ★★☆ **Complete the sentences about yourself with *used to* or *didn't use to*.**

When I was five, …

1 I _____ go to a different school.

2 my mum _____ wake me up at 7 am.

3 I _____ eat cereal for breakfast.

4 I _____ walk to school.

5 I _____ have a lot of homework.

6 my dad _____ read me a bedtime story every night.

8 ★★★ **Antonio is asking Elsa about her primary school. Write the questions. Then match them with the answers.**

0 Which / school / go / to
  *Which school did you use to go to?* [d]

1 wear / school uniform
  _____ ☐

2 have / a lot of homework
  _____ ☐

3 learn / English
  _____ ☐

4 learn / any other languages
  _____ ☐

5 What / favourite / subject
  _____ ☐

a It used to be Maths.

b Yes, I used to learn French.

c Yes, I used to be really good at it.

d I used to go to Middleham Primary School.

e No, I used to wear my ordinary clothes.

f No. Our teacher didn't use to give us much.

9 ★★☆ **In three of the sentences, you can use *would* or *wouldn't*. Tick them and rewrite them using *would*.**

1 I used to have curly hair. ☐
  _____
  _____

2 I used to play in the park every day after school. ☐
  _____
  _____

3 I didn't use to like cheese but now I do. ☐
  _____
  _____

4 I used to eat vegetables with each meal. ☐
  _____
  _____

5 I used to be very good at English. ☐
  _____
  _____

6 I used to go for a long bike ride every weekend. ☐
  _____
  _____

## GET IT RIGHT!

### *used to* and *usually*

**Learners sometimes confuse *used to* and *usually*. We use *used to* to refer to events which happened regularly in the past.**

✓ *When I was at college, I **used to** work in a clothes shop.*

**We use *usually* to refer to events which happen regularly in the present. We do not use *used to* for this.**

✓ *I **usually** go to the cinema on Wednesdays because it's cheaper.*

✗ *I used to go to the cinema on Wednesdays because it's cheaper.*

**Complete the sentences with *used to* or *usually* and the correct form of the verb in brackets.**

0 I _____*used to live*_____ (live) in a really small village and I really liked it.

1 We _____ (sing) in shows together when we were younger.

2 These days I _____ (go) to bed early.

3 They _____ (watch) TV on Wednesday evenings because that's when their favourite programme is on.

4 Could you give us the 10% discount that we _____ (get) in the past?

5 Rex is more attractive than he _____ (be).

6 Do you _____ (wear) that funny hat?

 # VOCABULARY
## Descriptive verbs

 → SB p.22

**1** ★☆☆ **Unscramble the words to make descriptive verbs.**

1 cefro _____
2 ssmha _____
3 ketris _____
4 gnreea _____
5 okhsc _____
6 ebg _____
7 osdliemh _____

**2** ★★☆ **Complete the sentences with the correct form of verbs from Exercise 1.**

0 Passengers were _enraged_ by the 90-minute delay to their flight.
1 The man _____ the window to rescue the boy from the fire.
2 The building was unsafe after the fire, so the council _____ it.
3 The young man _____ the woman not to leave him.
4 Our neighbours were _____ to find a burglar in their flat.
5 The police _____ the door open to enter the house.
6 Some cars were _____ by the falling tree.

**3** ★★☆ **Complete the crossword with synonyms of the underlined words.**

**ACROSS**
1 Don't push the window so hard. You'll break it!
7 They knocked down the old cinema and built a car park.

**DOWN**
2 The football fans were really angry when their team lost.
3 We asked him again and again to tell us the secret, but he refused.
4 No! We've broken the window!
5 It was lucky the ball didn't hit you on the head!
6 This news is going to be a bad surprise for everyone.

**4** ★★★ **Complete the information about a robbery with the correct form of the verbs from Exercise 1. Then number the events in the order they happened.**

☐ A The two men tried to ¹_____ the horse into the van. They pushed and pulled but it refused to go in.

☐ B First, Fred went to get the horse. He was ²_____ when he saw it because it was much bigger than he had thought. But he got on it and rode nervously out of the field.

☐ C Just then, a car appeared. A woman got out and ³_____ the men to stop. The horse recognised its owner immediately and waited quietly while she phoned the police.

☐ D It was a champion racehorse. Charlie and Fred had a brilliant plan: steal it and ask a million pounds for its return!

☐ E The horse was walking slowly down the road, but when it saw Charlie and the van, it started to run very fast. Fred ⁴_____ his head on a tree and nearly fell off.

☐ F The horse became so ⁵_____ that it ⁶_____ a window and nearly ⁷_____ the van!

**PRONUNCIATION**
Initial consonant clusters with /s/
Go to page 118.

## Time periods

→ SB p.25

**5** ★★☆ **Match the parts of the sentences.**

1 In this day and age, ☐
2 A decade ago, ☐
3 In the last century, ☐
4 In medieval times, ☐
5 From 1837 until 1901, ☐

a not many people had electric cars.
b there were two world wars.
c there was no electricity.
d most people have a smartphone.
e Queen Victoria was on the throne.

**6** ★★★ **Write your own sentences using the time phrases.**

1 In this day and age, _____
2 A decade ago, _____
3 In the last century, _____
4 Nowadays, _____
5 Not so long ago, _____
6 In medieval times, _____

# REFERENCE

in the last century

not so long ago    a decade ago

the recent past

from 2000 until 2020

a long, long time ago in history

Time periods

in the olden days

in medieval times

these days

the present

in this day and age

nowadays

## DESCRIPTIVE VERBS

beg

demolish

enrage

force

shock

smash

strike

# VOCABULARY *EXTRA*

**1  Match the parts of the sentences.**

1  A strong hurricane **destroyed**
2  Iona **endured** weeks
3  Two prisoners **escaped**
4  Firefighters **fought**
5  Oscar **screamed**
6  Everyone in the town **suffered**

a  'Help!'
b  to save the old building.
c  of pain after her accident.
d  after the earthquake.
e  the town.
f  during the night.

**2  Complete the table with the verbs in bold in Exercise 1.**

| Verbs to describe ... |
| --- |
| people's feelings |
| |
| |
| |
| actions |
| |
| |

**3  Complete the sentences. Choose the correct pairs of verbs in the list and write them in the correct form.**

destroy / suffer  |  endure / fight  |  escape / scream

1  The boys _____ for help while they _____ from the fire.
2  While the doctors _____ to save the boy's life, he _____ a lot of pain.
3  Many people _____ after their homes were _____ in the storm.

**4  Complete the sentences with your own ideas.**

1  I screamed when _____ .
2  I endured terrible pain when _____ .
3  In history, people suffered hardship when _____ .

# BAD TIMES, GOOD TIMES

My name is Henry Ackroyd. I was born in 1845 in Bradford, a town in the north of England. Bradford was well known for its wool <u>cloth</u>. Business was good, but industry polluted the town with smoke and industrial waste. Thick black smoke would pour out of hundreds of tall chimneys day and night, seven days a week. The town's drinking water came from a river full of industrial waste. Unsurprisingly, the people of the town suffered from bad health. Thousands of people used to die every year from <u>diseases</u> such as typhoid and cholera.

Like most other people, my parents moved to Bradford from the countryside to find work. These workers needed somewhere to live, so houses were built very quickly. They were close together with few windows and no heating. Families like mine would live in one small room with just one water <u>tap</u> at the end of the street. I remember the streets were full of rubbish and there were pigs and rats eating it. My parents endured long working hours in the factory – 12–15 hours a day – for very low pay.

Life was extremely hard until the day my father changed his job. He went to work in a factory that was owned by Mr Titus Salt. Soon after, Mr Salt, who owned four more factories, moved his business out of Bradford and built one enormous, modern factory on the River Aire. Nearby, he built 824 houses for his workers and their families. We were lucky enough to move to Saltaire! Can you see where the name came from?

Mr Salt was one of the few <u>factory owners</u> who understood that happy, healthy workers were good for business: they worked harder and produced more.

Life suddenly got better! My father, like all Mr Salt's workers, only used to work ten hours a day. We lived in a new house with bedrooms, a kitchen, a living room, a bathroom and a vegetable garden. Workers used to pay a <u>rent</u> of 12 percent of their weekly pay. The village also had shops, a wash-house, a library, clubs, a small hospital and an evening school for adults. Mr Salt believed in education and encouraged his workers to study and improve themselves. My sisters and I went to the village school – all the children had to go to school until they were 12. That was one of Saltaire's rules. Another one was that if workers lost their job, they lost their house, too. My parents were always telling us how lucky we were to live in Saltaire. Mr Salt wasn't the only factory owner with new ideas, but he certainly changed the lives of people like me and my family for the better. We were very fortunate!

## BRADFORD
### AND THE INDUSTRIAL REVOLUTION

**POPULATION**
**1801:** 13,000   **1851:** 104,000

**INDUSTRY:** WOOL FACTORIES
**1851:** 200 factories

**FAMOUS FOR:** wool cloth and pollution
Bradford was the most polluted town in England.

## READING

1 **Read the article quickly. Why were Henry Ackroyd and his family fortunate?**

2 **Read the article again and answer the questions.**

   1 Why was Bradford so polluted?
   _____

   2 What were the living conditions of most workers like?
   _____

   3 How did Henry Ackroyd's life change?
   _____

   4 In what ways was Titus Salt different from other factory owners at the time?
   _____

3 CRITICAL THINKING **Put the sentences in order according to the text.**

   ☐ A Mr Salt built one large factory in the countryside near the town.

   ☐ B Living and working conditions for Mr Salt's workers improved.

   ☐ C Bradford grew into a big industrial town with many problems.

   ☐ D Mr Salt's workers lived in a village near the factory.

   ☐ E Bradford was an ordinary small town.

   ☐ F Mr Salt had a number of cloth factories in Bradford.

4 **What do you think life was like for teenagers in these places? Choose either Bradford or Saltaire, and imagine you were living there in the 19th century. Write a paragraph describing your life.**

# DEVELOPING Writing

## A newspaper article

1  **INPUT**  **Read the article and complete the fact file.**

### Lost for 200 YEARS

**1**

**2** Imagine discovering that an old object in your house is in fact a valuable treasure! That is exactly what happened recently to a family in Edinburgh.

**3** A small statue of a man that the family had had for years was, in fact, one of the Isle of Lewis chessmen. Ninety-three chessmen had been found, buried on a beach on the Isle of Lewis, Scotland, in 1831. Five of the chessmen had been lost and this funny little statue was one of them! The chess set was probably made in the 12th century in Norway from the teeth of whales and walruses. It is now one of the most popular displays at the British Museum, London.

**4** The chessman had belonged to the family since their grandfather gave it to them. His daughter loved the statue and she used to keep it in a special bag. From time to time, she would take it out and look at it because she liked the funny little man.

**5** The family realised that the statue was very old and had often wondered what it was and where it had come from. Not long ago, they showed it to an antiques expert. As they were unwrapping it, the expert immediately recognised it as one of the missing chessmen from the Isle of Lewis in Scotland. But that wasn't the only shock. The expert told them the statue that their grandfather had bought for £5 in 1964 is now worth about a million pounds!

2  **ANALYSE**  **Match the parts of the article (1–5) with the descriptions (A–E).**

A The lead sentence – a short introduction  ☐
B The discovery – what's happening to the chessmen now  ☐
C The headline  ☐
D The story of how the family got the chessman  ☐
E Background information about the chessmen  ☐

3  **PLAN**  **Think about an interesting discovery in your town or country. It can be real or imaginary. Make a plan using these questions.**

- What was discovered? _____
- Where was it discovered? _____
- Why is it important? _____
- How was it discovered? _____
- What's happening to the object now? _____

4  **PRODUCE**  **Write an article for your school newspaper about an interesting discovery in your town (200–250 words). Use your plan from Exercise 3. Make sure you include all the points in the checklist.**

✔ CHECKLIST

☐ Think of an eye-catching headline.
☐ Use past tenses appropriately.
☐ Check spelling and punctuation.

## LISTENING

**1** 🔊 2.02 **Listen to a conversation about schools in the 19th century. Which subjects did children use to have to study?**

A Maths, Reading and Writing
B Maths, Chemistry and Physics
C Reading, Writing and Geography

**2** 🔊 2.02 **Listen again and match the parts of the sentences.**

1 Before 1870, only boys ☐
2 After 1870, all children ☐
3 They used to have separate ☐
4 They didn't use to have any ☐
5 In the olden days, not many men ☐
6 They didn't use to have Geography ☐
7 They used to finish school ☐
8 They used to have a two-hour lunch break ☐

a playgrounds for boys and girls.
b at 5 pm.
c posters on the walls.
d used to go to school.
e so they could walk home for lunch.
f used to become teachers.
g aged 5–13 used to go to school.
h lessons at school.

## DIALOGUE

**3** **Put the sentences in order to make a conversation between a mother and her son.**

☐ Mum No, the Millennium Bridge didn't use to be here either.
☐ Mum Yes, it did. It used to be an old power station.
[1] Mum I used to walk along here every afternoon after school.
☐ Mum It's completely changed. The Globe Theatre didn't use to be here.
☐ Mum That's the Tate Modern. It's a big modern art gallery.
☐ Son And what's that huge building over there?
☐ Son Did it always use to look like that?
☐ Son Didn't it? What about this bridge?
☐ Son Lucky you, Mum! Has much changed?

**4** **Complete the dialogues with the phrases in the list.**

> in those days | school dinners
> the other children | use to watch
> would play football | your favourite meal

**1**

Tanya What did you use to do after school?
Dad I would meet up with _____ in the neighbourhood. If it was raining, we would play board games indoors. When the weather was nice, we _____ in the park.

**2**

Ricky What kind of programmes did you _____ , Grandma?
Grandma I liked programmes about pop music. _____ , there used to be a show every Saturday with the new songs of the week. They'd often have the band in the studio playing their song. That was my favourite!

**3**

Tim Did you use to take a packed lunch to school, Mum?
Mum No, I didn't. We used to get _____ . The menu was the same every week or every two weeks. I can still remember every single meal.

**4**

Carlos What was _____ ?
Mum Well, I can tell you my least favourite meal – a slice of beef, cabbage and mashed potato.

# TOWARDS B2 First for Schools

 **SPEAKING**
Interview

## EXAM GUIDE

**For this part of the test, there will be two examiners and two candidates in the room. You will talk to one of the examiners (the interlocutor). The other examiner (the assessor) will just listen. The examiner will ask you short questions about your everyday life and personal experiences. Candidates interact individually with the examiner. The examiner speaks to the candidates alternately.**

- Give a short but complete answer to each question.
- If you don't hear or don't understand the question, ask the examiner to repeat it.

First, the examiner will say:

*Good morning / afternoon / evening.*

*My name is ... and this is my colleague ... .*

*And your names are?*

*Where are you from?*

*First, we'd like to know something about you.*

Then the examiner will ask you two or three questions on topics such as:

- family
- holidays
- future plans.

1 **Match the questions with the topics above.**

1 Are you going to do anything exciting soon? _____

2 Who are you most like in your family? Tell me about him / her. _____

3 What's the best holiday you've ever been on? _____

4 Tell us about a person in your family that you enjoy spending time with. _____

5 What do you think you will be doing in 10 years' time? _____

6 How do you like to spend time with your family? _____

7 Do you think English will be useful in your future work? _____

8 Tell us about a holiday you've really enjoyed. _____

9 Where would you like to go for your next holiday? Why? _____

2 ◁) 2.03 **Listen to an interview with two candidates and write the question numbers.**

1 Katya answered questions _____ and _____ .

2 Alexei answered questions _____ and _____ .

3 ◁) 2.03 **How well did they do? Listen again and grade the candidates' performance.**

\* = quite good   \*\* = good   \*\*\* = very good

|  | Katya | Alexei |
|---|---|---|
| 1 easy to understand |  |  |
| 2 answered the questions |  |  |
| 3 good vocabulary |  |  |

4 **Imagine you are an exam candidate. Answer the questions in Exercise 1.**

# CONSOLIDATION

## 🎧 LISTENING

1 🔊 2.04 **Listen and circle the correct option: A, B or C.**

1 How does Isabel feel about her future?
   A frightened
   B confident
   C optimistic

2 What do Jack and Isabel agree about?
   A They're looking forward to university.
   B It's easy to start a career nowadays.
   C There's a wide range of university courses.

3 Jack and Isabel think their parents had
   A very little careers advice at their schools.
   B a lot of help preparing for their future careers.
   C the opportunity to study interesting subjects.

2 🔊 2.04 **Listen again and answer the questions.**

1 What is Jack looking forward to?
   _____

2 What's Isabel's main problem?
   _____

3 Why does Jack think life was easier for their parents?
   _____

4 What is a careers advisor?
   _____

5 What advice does Jack give Isabel?
   _____

## © GRAMMAR

3 **Circle the correct options.**

1 I *go* / *'m going* for a walk in the park every weekend.
2 Max and I *go* / *are going* for a walk tomorrow morning.
3 When I arrived, the place was empty – everyone *went* / *had gone* home.
4 I used to *going* / *go* and play by the river every day.
5 In the future, life *is being* / *will be* very different from today.
6 The film finished, so then I *had gone* / *went* to bed.
7 Tomorrow I'*m meeting* / *meet* my friends in town.
8 Many years ago, my family *would* / *used to* live in a very small flat.

## 🄰 VOCABULARY

4 **Complete each sentence with one word.**

1 In this _____ and age, almost everyone knows how to use a computer.
2 I've _____ a resolution to never eat chocolate again.
3 She only started work here last month, but she's already got _____ .
4 I want to travel – I don't want to get married and settle _____ .
5 Is this film from 2014 or 2015? Well, it's from about a _____ ago, anyway.
6 He went to university and got a _____ in Mathematics.
7 Look! There's a broken window. Who _____ the glass?
8 As you get older, it becomes harder to _____ your ways.
9 The house was old and dangerous, so the city council _____ it.
10 The post office said it could take _____ to two weeks to deliver the package.

5 **Match the parts of the sentences.**

1 When he reached the age of 63, ☐
2 We'd forgotten our keys, ☐
3 They were shocked ☐
4 When she stopped working, ☐
5 They're only 20 but they've decided ☐
6 She decided to start a career ☐
7 It isn't a good idea to get into ☐
8 My friend didn't do very ☐
9 It's up to you – ☐
10 People don't write many letters ☐

a by the monsters in the horror film.
b well in the exam, unfortunately.
c in banking.
d nowadays.
e he decided to retire from his job.
f she took up photography.
g you decide.
h the habit of eating a lot of fast food.
i so we smashed the window and climbed in.
j to settle down and start a family.

## DIALOGUE

**6** 🔊 2.05 **Complete the dialogue with the phrases in the list.**

> don't be silly | where shall I start
> now you mention it | you're a star
> stuff like that | here we go
> where have you been hiding | what's up

**Johnny** Hi, Sofia! I haven't seen you for ages.
¹_____ ?

**Sofia** Hi, Johnny. Yes, I'm sorry. I've just had so much to do lately.

**Johnny** Oh, ²_____ with the excuses. Like what?

**Sofia** Oh, well, ³_____ ? Like, revising for exams, taking care of my brother …
⁴_____ .

**Johnny** Your brother? ⁵_____ with him?

**Sofia** Didn't you hear? He had a pretty bad accident a few weeks ago. He was in hospital for over two weeks. He's home now. I have to look after him in the afternoon when I get back from school.

**Johnny** Wow, Sofia. I'm sorry to hear that.
⁶_____ . I don't know how you manage to look after someone who's ill.

**Sofia** Oh, ⁷_____ . There isn't much to manage really – but he can't move around much, so I just have to get food and things, help him get dressed, stuff like that. Anyway, he's my brother, so I want to help him. I'm sure you've helped people in your family, too.

**Johnny** Well, ⁸_____ , I helped to look after my dad when he was ill a few years ago.

**Sofia** See? We all do things when we have to. And that's what I'm doing. It is tiring, though.

## 📖 READING

**7** **Read the article and mark the sentences T (true) or F (false). Then correct the false sentences.**

### *Charles Dickens and* 'Hard Times'

Charles Dickens was one of the most famous and successful writers in England during the 19th century. He became very wealthy and travelled to the US twice to give talks. His books are still popular today and many have been made into films – *Great Expectations*, *Oliver Twist* and *A Christmas Carol* are perhaps the best-known examples.

But Dickens' life was not always an easy one, especially when he was a small boy. His parents had serious money problems. When disaster struck, Charles had only just turned 12 years old. He had to leave school to start work to earn enough money for his family to live on. He got a job in a factory where he had to stick labels onto bottles full of 'blacking', a polish for cleaning shoes. He was paid six shillings a week – that's about £12.50 a week in today's money. He hated the factory and the work, but the experience changed his life and inspired his career as a writer.

A short time later, his father was sent to prison because he owed money – this happened to many people at that time. Then the family house was sold, and Charles' mother, brothers and sisters went to live in the prison, too. Charles never forgot this period of his life. As an adult, he wanted people to know about the terrible conditions that children often had to work in. And when he started writing, his stories were full of people who suffered the things that he had gone through himself. In fact, one of his novels is called *Hard Times*.

1 Charles Dickens' work is mostly forgotten today. ☐
2 Charles had to go to work to help his family. ☐
3 Charles was almost 13 when he went to work in the factory. ☐
4 Charles' job was to polish shoes. ☐
5 The whole Dickens family was sent to prison. ☐
6 In his later life, Charles wanted to help improve the situation for children. ☐

## ✏️ WRITING

**8** **Write a short description (150–200 words). Imagine you are 12-year-old Charles Dickens, working in the factory. Say what your work is like and how you feel.**

# 3 WHAT'S IN A NAME?

## Ⓖ GRAMMAR
*(don't) have to / ought to / should(n't) / must*

→ SB p.32

1 ⭐☆☆ **Look at the pictures and complete the sentences with the phrases in the list.**

> ask someone | be so shy | buy a hairbrush | go and see it
> go to bed so late | wear something warmer

1 You should _____ .

2 He shouldn't _____ .

3 I must _____ .

4 I shouldn't _____ .

5 We ought to _____ .

6 We must _____ .

2 ⭐⭐☆ **Circle the correct options.**

1 It's a holiday tomorrow. We *have to / don't have to* go to school.

2 Well, it's your party. You *have to / don't have to* invite people you don't like.

3 Coffee isn't free here. You *have to / don't have to* pay for it.

4 Just your first name is OK. You *have to / don't have to* write your full name.

5 Well, those are the rules – you *have to / don't have to* be 16 to be allowed in.

3 ⭐⭐☆ **Complete the conversation with *have to / has to / don't have to / doesn't have to.***

**Joe** Why do I ¹_____ go to bed now? Helen ²_____ , and she's only two years older than me.

**Dad** That's right. But Helen ³_____ get up at seven o'clock to go to school. You do.

**Joe** Only because you say so. It only takes me 15 minutes to get dressed and have breakfast.

**Mum** But you ⁴_____ have a shower, too, remember.

**Joe** OK, 20 minutes. But I ⁵_____ leave the house until 7.50. So, I could get up at 7.30. And so, I ⁶_____ go to bed now.

**Mum** All right, but remember – it's me who ⁷_____ deal with you when you're tired and irritable in the morning!

4 ⭐⭐⭐ **Complete the sentences with the correct form of *have to* and a suitable verb.**

1 I'm going to a wedding tomorrow, so no T-shirt for me! I _____ a suit and tie.

2 Rory, if you're going skateboarding, you _____ in the park and not go on the road.

3 Lucy can't come out with us tonight – she _____ her baby sister.

4 In some countries, you can eat with your hands – you _____ with a knife and fork.

5 Lottie's got a well-paid job, so she _____ about money.

6 Well, if you want better grades, you _____ more.

7 We _____ the dishes – we can put them all in the dishwasher.

8 My sister and I have each got a laptop now, so we _____ one any more.

*had better (not)* → SB p.33

**5** ★☆☆ **Match the parts of the sentences.**

1 We mustn't be late, so ☐
2 This food isn't very fresh, so ☐
3 You've already spent a lot of money, so ☐
4 It's probably going to be cold, so ☐
5 My eyes are getting tired, so ☐
6 The children didn't understand the rules, so ☐
7 I don't think the water in that bottle is clean, so ☐
8 I hate it when you call me names, so ☐

a I'd better wear a jumper.
b we'd better leave now.
c you'd better explain them again.
d we'd better not drink it.
e you'd better throw it away.
f you'd better not do it again.
g you'd better not buy anything else.
h I'd better not look at a screen any more.

**6** ★★☆ **Complete each dialogue with *'d better / 'd better not* and a verb from the list.**

> apologise | call | eat | stay
> study | tell | turn | wear

1 **A** We've got a test tomorrow.
  **B** Well, you _____ , tonight, then.
2 **A** My parents get worried if I get home late.
  **B** OK, we _____ too long at the party, then.
3 **A** I think he's quite upset about what I said.
  **B** You _____ , then.
4 **A** I've got tickets for the concert tonight.
  **B** Well, you _____ Harry. He couldn't get one, so he'd be envious.
5 **A** I don't feel too well.
  **B** Well, you _____ any more crisps, then.
6 **A** Look! That man's fallen over. I think he's ill.
  **B** We _____ an ambulance right away.
7 **A** The neighbours are complaining about the noise.
  **B** Oh, OK. We _____ the music down a bit.
8 **A** It's a very special party tomorrow night.
  **B** Yes, I know. We _____ something nice.

*can('t) / must(n't)* → SB p.35

**7** ★☆☆ **Complete the meaning of each sign. Use *can / can't* or *mustn't* and a verb, where necessary.**

1 You _____ turn right.

4 You _____ take photos here.

2 You _____ park here.

5 You _____ here.

3 You _____ go in here.

6 You _____ your phone here.

## GET IT *RIGHT!*

**Confusion between *could* and *should***

We use *should* to indicate that something is a good idea or that something will happen under normal circumstances.

We use *could* to indicate that something may be true or possible.

✓ If you want, you **could** bring some drinks.
✗ If you want, you should bring some drinks.

**Circle the correct modal verb.**

0 Two hours ~~should~~ / could be enough to do everything. That's how long it normally takes.
1 I would like to ask if I *should / could* have another month to finish the project.
2 If you want to get healthier, you *should / could* eat balanced meals.
3 On the other hand, there *should / could* be risks with that plan.
4 *Should / Could* you please consider my application and look at my case?
5 I think that we *should / could* take the route around Lake Frene.
6 Martha did not know whether she *should / could* tell the police or not.

## VOCABULARY
### Making and selling
→ SB p.32

1 ★★☆ **Complete the phrases.**

advertisement | brand | chain
consumer | image | logo
manufacturer | product

1 a _____ of shops
2 a _____ of doors and windows
3 the _____ that a company makes
4 an _____ in a magazine or on TV
5 the _____ that people prefer to buy
6 the _____ that a company uses to identify its products
7 an _____ that a company creates in consumers' minds
8 a _____ who buys goods or services

2 ★★☆ **Circle the correct words.**

1 This shop is one of a *brand / chain* – there are over 30 in this country.
2 I love that company's new TV *logo / advertisement*.
3 Some of the best-known car *manufacturers / products* are Korean.
4 The marketing department designed a new *image / logo* to put on their products.
5 Our company is launching a new *brand / product* next week.
6 Many companies support a charity – it improves their *consumer / image*.

> **PRONUNCIATION**
> Strong and weak forms: /ɒv/ and /əv/
> Go to page 118.

### Expressions with *name*
→ SB p.35

3 ★★☆ **Complete the sentences with expressions with *name*.**

1 I eat everything – _____ , and I'll eat it!
2 Nobody knew Petra Tomes ten years ago, but she soon _____ for herself as an athlete.
3 They're engaged to be married, but they haven't _____ yet.
4 You've probably never heard of Peter Gene Hernandez, but his _____ is Bruno Mars.
5 Go and talk to that boy – um, _____ , you know, the new guy.
6 Well, if you want to be successful, you have to work hard – sorry, but that's _____ .
7 It's so childish, I think, when kids at school _____ other kids _____ .
8 Everyone knows who Lilian Rainey is – she's a _____ in this country!

4 ★★☆ **Find eight words in the wordsearch. Then use them to complete the sentences.**

| E | B | S | K | Q | U | R | W |
|---|---|---|---|---|---|---|---|
| K | I | T | D | B | W | E | Y |
| A | G | A | M | E | A | L | Q |
| M | I | G | R | F | D | H | M |
| P | O | E | L | L | A | C | E |
| W | H | A | T | X | Y | U | R |
| T | S | O | Y | L | P | A | J |

1 My cousin's got loads of video games. You name _____ , he's got it!
2 Tallulah's a great singer. She's sure to _____ a name for herself in music.
3 We don't know when the party is. We're waiting for Kelly to name the _____ .
4 Oh! I've just seen _____'s-her-name. I can never remember what she's called!
5 Say sorry. It isn't nice to _____ people names.
6 Elvis Cool isn't his real name. It's only his _____ name.
7 It's my favourite brand and it's a _____ name in sportswear.
8 You have to train hard if you want to be in the team. It's the name of the _____ .

5 ★★★ **Answer the questions about yourself.**

1 Which brand logos do you like? Why?
_____

2 What is your favourite brand of clothes? Why?
_____

3 What is your favourite advertisement? Why?
_____

4 Who has made a name for themselves in your country recently and why?
_____

5 Who is the biggest name in sport in your country?
_____

6 What are the most popular chains of shops in your country?
_____

# REFERENCE

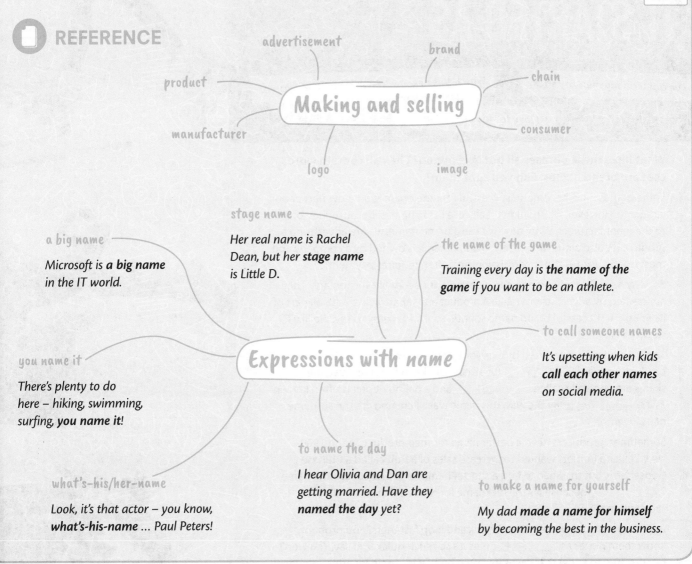

**Making and selling**
- advertisement
- product
- manufacturer
- brand
- chain
- consumer
- logo
- image

**Expressions with name**

*stage name*
Her real name is Rachel Dean, but her **stage name** is Little D.

*a big name*
Microsoft is **a big name** in the IT world.

*the name of the game*
Training every day is **the name of the game** if you want to be an athlete.

*to call someone names*
It's upsetting when kids **call each other names** on social media.

*you name it*
There's plenty to do here – hiking, swimming, surfing, **you name it!**

*to name the day*
I hear Olivia and Dan are getting married. Have they **named the day** yet?

*to make a name for yourself*
My dad **made a name for himself** by becoming the best in the business.

*what's-his/her-name*
Look, it's that actor – you know, **what's-his-name** … Paul Peters!

 VOCABULARY *EXTRA*

**1 Circle the correct words.**

1 A *competitor / consumer* is another business that makes or sells the same products as your company.
2 Washing machines, fridges and televisions are examples of electrical *manufacturers / goods*.
3 A house is usually the biggest *purchase / product* a person makes in their life.
4 You can save money if you wait to buy things in a *chain / sale*.
5 There's a weekly market with hundreds of different *shops / stalls*.

**2 Complete the mind map with words from Exercise 1 and the Reference section. Sometimes several answers are possible.**

manufacturer

**Making and selling**
- making
- brand
- advertising
- selling
- logo

**3 Write examples of shops, products and brands that you know.**

1 Manufacturers:
_____
_____

2 Electrical goods:
_____
_____

3 Chains:
_____
_____

4 Your favourite market and its stalls:
_____
_____

31

# IT STARTED AS A BRAND

I've got it on my memory stick.

Watch this new trick I can do with my yo-yo!

I'd love to ride on a Jet Ski!

_____

_____

_____

**What have these phrases all got in common? They all contain words that are brand names. Can you spot them?**

Some brands have become so successful that their names are now part of our language. However, we shouldn't really use these names, because they belong to the manufacturers. Every time we use a brand name, we are advertising a product. It's also a question of law: a brand name is owned by a company and must not be used without permission, and often requires payment!

So, why have so many brand names entered our everyday vocabulary? They are created by advertisers to make a product appear attractive – it's all part of its image. A successful brand name sounds cool and is easy to say. We like it, so we use it!

Some brand names are used by everyone to include all types of the same product, such as [1]_____ for all cola drinks. In the same way, inline skates are generally called [2]_____ and a ballpoint pen is often known as a [3]_____ . By the way, this name wasn't created, it's the surname of its inventor!

Sometimes, producers need a better name for their product. In the 1960s, New Zealand farmers wanted to increase sales of a fruit called a Chinese Gooseberry, but they had to find a shorter name for it. They chose the name [4]_____ because it's the nickname for New Zealanders and the name of their national bird.

Also, where would we be without hook and loop fasteners? You probably know them better as [5]_____ as it's so much quicker to say. You won't be surprised to know that it was invented by a Swiss engineer after he noticed how bits of sticks and leaves stuck to his dog's fur during walks in the forest!

What about all the new inventions that haven't already got a name? A new product appears and because it's the first one in existence, people only know it by its brand name. This is what happened for the first moving staircase or [6]_____ and many toys and games, such as the [7]_____ ! So, we shouldn't call every flying plastic disc by this name. Interestingly, this game was invented by a group of American students using a metal pie plate – ouch!

## READING

1 **Read the article quickly and write the name of the products under the photos.**

2 **Complete the article with the brand names in the list.**

> biro | coke | escalator | frisbee
> kiwi | rollerblades | velcro

3 **Read the article again. Choose the correct words.**

1 If you want to use a brand name, you should *ask / tell* the owner of the brand.

2 The brand name is an important part of a product's *advertisement / image*.

3 We use brand names in everyday language because we like the *words / products*.

4 **CRITICAL THINKING Choose the best option (A, B or C).**

1 What is the purpose of the text?

A to advertise certain products

B to explain the origins of words

C to explain the laws of brand names

5 **Tick the sentences that are true for you.**

- I learned something new. ☐
- The text was interesting. ☐
- This information could be useful. ☐
- I can apply this to other situations. ☐

6 **Do some research to find other brand names that have become part of everyday vocabulary in English and in your language. Write a short paragraph about one of them.**

## An email reply

**1** INPUT **Read the email. What does Zehra want to know?** _____

**Zehra**
FloraH@mailme.com
Re: Exchange visit!

Hi Flora!

My name's Zehra and I'm coming to your school on an exchange visit next month. I'm really excited about it – hope you are, too!

Why am I writing this right now? The thing is, I really don't want to do the wrong thing while I'm there, especially at school. So I'm wondering if you could tell me a bit about it, like, what are the rules? About phones, clothes, talking in class, food … you know what I mean, don't you?

Could you send me a quick email to tell me?

Take care and hope to hear from you soon.

Zehra

**Flora**
ZehraP@mailme.com
Re: Exchange visit!

Hi there, Zehra!

Thanks for your email – great to hear from you. Yes, I'm looking forward to the exchange, too!

Anyway, about the rules. The school here isn't very strict about most things, but there are a few things you should know. First of all – clothes. We haven't got a uniform, so you can wear what you want, but we can't wear jeans with holes in them or anything like that, or T-shirts with writing on them. You should wear things that are comfortable. Oh, and it'll be kind of cold when you're here, so you'd better bring some warm clothes, OK?

The school's pretty strict about phones. Of course, you can bring them, but you have to switch them off in lessons – you can't just put them on silent. You can bring food to school, but you must eat it outside during the break – except if it's raining. Then, you can eat in the classroom (but not in the corridors!).

Not much else to say – I mean, it's a normal school and the teachers are mostly kind of normal, too – so no stress! You really don't have to worry about anything else.

Hope this helps. Write again soon and tell me if there's anything else you need to know.

Love,

Flora

**2** **Read Flora's reply and mark the sentences T (true) or F (false). Then correct the false sentences.**

1 Flora gives all the information Zehra asked for. ☐
2 Students don't have to wear a uniform at Flora's school. ☐
3 Students can wear any clothes they like. ☐
4 Students must not take their phones into class. ☐

**3** ANALYSE **Answer the questions about informal language in the emails.**

Flora writes: '… you'd better bring some warm clothes, OK?'

1 She uses the word 'OK' to *check for understanding / show disagreement.*

2 What does Zehra use instead of 'OK' to do this?

_____

Flora writes: 'it'll be kind of cold when you're here.'

3 'kind of' means *very / a bit.*

4 Find and underline another time when Flora writes 'kind of' in her email.

Flora writes: '… great to hear from you.'

5 She has left out the words *This is / It is.*

6 Find two other times when she leaves words out. What are the missing words? _____

**4** PLAN **Imagine that Zehra wrote her email to you. Plan your reply to her.**

Think about the rules in your school and the things Zehra asks. Make notes about:

- clothes
- food
- phones
- talking in class
- other rules Zehra should know about

**5** PRODUCE **Write your reply to Zehra (200–250 words). Use your plan from Exercise 4. Make sure you include all the points in the checklist.**

## ✓ CHECKLIST

Start with a friendly greeting.

Answer all Zehra's questions and tell her about any other rules.

Use an informal style with short sentences, short forms of verbs (*it's, I'm, that's*), direct questions and short phrases, such as *you know, right? OK, Yeah.*

End the email in a friendly way and offer to give Zehra more information if she needs it.

# LISTENING

1 🔊 3.02 **Listen to a conversation between Annie, Ben and the new girl. Choose the correct answer (A, B or C).**

1 The new girl's name is …
   A Maureen.    B Morgan.    C Morwenna.
2 She is from …
   A Cornwall.    B Wales.    C London.
3 She says that in Cornwall …
   A there is nothing to do.
   B some names have strange pronunciations.
   C the beaches aren't very nice.

2 🔊 3.02 **Listen again and mark the statements T (true) or F (false).**

1 Annie asks Morwenna to repeat her name. ☐
2 The name Morwenna is Welsh. ☐
3 Part of Morwenna's family lives in Cornwall. ☐
4 Morwenna says Newquay is a good place for surfing. ☐
5 The water in Newquay is warm. ☐
6 Ben pronounces Mousehole correctly. ☐
7 People in Cornwall don't mind if names are pronounced wrongly. ☐
8 Annie gets Morwenna's name wrong again. ☐

3 🔊 3.02 **Listen again. Complete the parts of the conversation.**

**1**

| | |
|---|---|
| Annie | I've never been there. Cornwall, I mean, but I'd really like to go. |
| Morwenna | Oh, ¹_____ . It's really nice. We go quite often – my mum's got family down there. In Penzance. |
| Ben | Anything to do there? |
| Morwenna | Sure – there are nice beaches and if you like surfing, ²_____ Newquay. |
| Annie | But isn't the water really cold? |
| Morwenna | Well, yes! So if you go surfing, ³_____ a wetsuit to keep warm in the water. |

**2**

| | |
|---|---|
| Morwenna | Yeah, really. If you go to Cornwall, ⁴_____ how to pronounce the names. Local people don't like it when tourists say the names wrong. |
| Annie | I guess not. |
| Ben | I think Annie's right – ⁵_____ a new brain. |
| Morwenna | Sorry? |
| Ben | Listen, ⁶_____ back. The next lesson starts in a few minutes. |

---

UK

Newquay    CORNWALL

Penzance
Mousehole

## DIALOGUE

4 **Complete the dialogues.**

> 'd better learn | 'd better take
> should know | should visit

**1**

A You live in Vancouver, don't you? I've always wanted to go there.
B That's right. And if you ever go there, you ¹_____ Stanley Park. It's beautiful!
A Is the weather nice there?
B Well, it can be OK in summer – but it rains quite a lot, so you ²_____ an umbrella!

**2**

A You live in Hamburg, right? I've always wanted to go there.
B Yes, I do. If you come, you should go and see the Miniature Wonderland. It's fantastic.
A Do you think I ³_____ German before I go?
B Well, you ⁴_____ a few words, I guess – but lots of people speak English, so you don't have to worry too much.

5 **Write a dialogue between you and a friend.**

The friend begins: 'You live in (name of your town / city), right? I've always wanted to go there.'
Give the friend some advice about where to go, what to see and what to do.
Use the dialogues in Exercise 4 to help you.

# TOWARDS B2 First for Schools

## 🎧 LISTENING
### Multiple choice

### EXAM GUIDE

**You will listen to eight different recordings. The eight recordings are a mix of short monologues and dialogues. For each one, there is a three-option multiple-choice question to answer. The questions tend to focus on gist, detail, purpose, attitude and opinion. You hear each recording twice.**

- Before you listen, read the context sentence (the question and the three options, A, B and C). This will give you a general idea of what you will hear.
- Listen carefully. Remember, you will <u>not</u> hear the same words as in the options, so listen for synonyms, paraphrases and expressions with a similar meaning.
- When the question asks you to understand a speaker's attitude or opinion, you need to form an impression by listening to the whole recording.

1   🔊 3.03   **You will hear people talking in eight different situations. For questions 1–8, choose the best answer (A, B or C).**

1  You hear a conversation in a shop. What is the problem with the shoes?
   A His wife doesn't like them.
   B He doesn't think they're right for him.
   C They're too small for him.

2  You hear a girl talking about puzzles. What does she say about them?
   A The puzzles are always easy to do.
   B She always solves the puzzles.
   C They develop her thinking abilities.

3  You hear a man telling a friend about a trip he made to China. What does he say about Shanghai?
   A It was amazing.
   B He spent seven days there.
   C He didn't see it.

4  You hear a woman telling a friend about her journey to work. How does she usually travel?
   A by car
   B by bike
   C by bus

5  You hear two teenagers talking about school. Why did the girl change schools?
   A Her old school was too far away.
   B She wanted to work harder.
   C Her parents decided for her.

6  You hear part of a radio interview with a man. What does the man do?
   A He writes poetry.
   B He's a singer in a band.
   C He writes the words for songs.

7  You hear a woman talking about her hobby. How does she feel while she is birdwatching?
   A tired
   B hopeful
   C excited

8  You hear a boy who wants to be a chef. How did he first become interested in cooking?
   A He tasted some excellent food in a restaurant.
   B He enjoyed cooking dinner for himself.
   C His mum cooked him a special birthday dinner.

# 4 WHAT WOULD YOU DO?

Grammar rap!

 **GRAMMAR**

### First and second conditional (review)
→ SB p.40

**1** ⭐☆☆ **Match the sentences with the pictures.**

 A

 C

 B

 D

1 If we lose this game, I won't be happy.
2 If we lost this game, I'd be very surprised.
3 If it snows tomorrow, we won't have to go to school.
4 If it snowed here, it would be very strange.

**2** ⭐⭐☆ **Complete the sentences with the correct form of the verbs in brackets to make first or second conditional sentences.**

0 I ___will tell___ (tell) you my secret if you ___promise___ (promise) not to tell anyone.

1 Be careful. The cat _____ (bite) you if you _____ (touch) it.

2 If Nils _____ (be) taller, he _____ (be) a really good basketball player.

3 If you _____ (meet) the president, _____ (you / ask) her to do something about climate change?

4 Hurry up, Molly! If we _____ (not leave) now, you _____ (miss) the train.

5 If I _____ (know) the answer, I still _____ (not tell) you.

6 If those students _____ (not stop) talking now, the teacher _____ (get) angry with the whole class.

7 _____ (you / be) scared if we _____ (meet) a bear in the woods?

8 Our team is the best. I _____ (be) very surprised if we _____ (not win).

**3** ⭐⭐☆ **Complete the sentences with the correct form of the verbs in brackets to make second conditional sentences.**

What [1]_____ you _____ (do) if you found an envelope full of money in the street? [2]_____ you _____ (take) it to the police station? Or [3]_____ you _____ (keep) it and buy yourself something you really wanted? [4]_____ you _____ (buy) your mum and dad a present? If you [5]_____ (buy) them a present, they [6]_____ (want) to know where you got the money from. If you [7]_____ (tell) them the truth, maybe they [8]_____ (not be) so happy. And if you [9]_____ (not tell) them the truth, you [10]_____ (feel) really bad. You know what, I hope I never find an envelope full of money in the street!

### Time conjunctions
→ SB p.40

**4** ⭐☆☆ **Circle the correct options.**

1 Grace is going to get a new computer *when / unless* she has enough money.
2 I'll phone you *until / as soon as* she leaves.
3 We'll start the meeting *until / when* Mr Benson arrives.
4 *If / Until* I don't pass my English test, I'll take it again.
5 You won't pass your driving test *if / unless* you practise more.
6 We'll watch the game *as soon as / until* half time.

**5** ⭐⭐☆ **Complete the sentences with *if, unless, until* or *as soon as*.**

1 _____ we hurry up, we'll be late for the party.
2 Jeremy's got the tickets, so we'll have to wait _____ he gets there before we can get in.
3 What will you do _____ we don't get any homework this weekend?
4 Maxine can't talk because she's in the shower. She'll call you _____ she gets out.
5 I'm seeing Shaun tonight, so I'll ask him _____ I see him.
6 _____ we can't get tickets, we can just watch the match on TV at my house.
7 I've got to go to the shops. Can you look after the baby _____ I get back?
8 I can't go to the party _____ I finish my project by Friday.

## *wish* and *if only*

→ SB p.41

**6** ★☆☆ **Circle the correct words.**

1 My mum wishes she *has* / *had* more time.

2 Rose wishes she *can* / *could* go to the theatre tonight.

3 If only the neighbour's dog *won't* / *wouldn't* bark all day.

4 The teacher wishes her students *weren't* / *aren't* so noisy.

5 If only I *am* / *was* taller.

6 Logan wishes Kirsty *will* / *would* talk to him.

7 If only we *could* / *can* play the piano.

**7** ★★☆ **Read the sentences. Write Julia's wishes.**

0 'My sister keeps taking my clothes.'
I wish *my sister wouldn't keep taking my clothes.*

1 'I don't understand Maths.'
If only _____

2 'The girls in my class are so childish.'
I wish _____

3 'I can't find my phone. Where is it?'
I wish _____

4 'I can't afford to buy those new shoes.'
If only _____

5 'We want to go to the concert, but the tickets are sold out.'
I wish _____

6 'We've got too much homework this weekend.'
If only _____

## Third conditional (review)

→ SB p.42

**8** ★☆☆ **Match the parts of the sentences.**

1 We wouldn't have watched the film ☐

2 I would have got a much better mark ☐

3 We would have saved a lot of money ☐

4 She would have got completely lost ☐

5 If you hadn't kicked the ball so hard, ☐

6 If Teresa had apologised, ☐

7 If I had had Finley's number, ☐

8 If the children had been a bit quieter, ☐

a if I'd studied harder.

b if she hadn't used the map on her phone.

c it wouldn't have knocked my glasses off.

d I would have sent him a message.

e if we had known it was so long and slow.

f they wouldn't have woken the baby.

g I would have forgiven her.

h if we'd eaten at home.

**9** ★★☆ **Read the story. Then complete the sentences with the correct form of the verbs in brackets.**

My friend Nathan threw a pen by mistake and it hit the teacher. The teacher was angry. Nathan didn't say anything. The teacher thought it was me and gave me detention. I went to detention and met a girl called Andrea. I asked her over to my place and she said yes. Now Andrea's my best friend.

0 If Nathan ___*hadn't thrown*___ a pen, it ___*wouldn't have hit*___ the teacher. (throw / hit)

1 If Nathan _____ honest, he _____ to detention. (be / go)

2 If I _____ to detention, I _____ Andrea. (go / meet)

3 If I _____ Andrea, I _____ invite her to my house. (meet / be able to)

4 If she _____ no to my invitation, I _____ at home alone. (say / stay)

5 If she _____ to my place, we _____ best friends. (come / become)

## GET IT RIGHT!

### *would have* + past participle

**Learners sometimes underuse *would have* + past participle, or use it in the *if*-clause where the past perfect tense is required.**

✓ *After the musical, we **would have gone** to a restaurant, but we didn't have time.*

✗ *After the musical, we ~~would go~~ to a restaurant, but we didn't have time.*

✓ *We would have appreciated it if you **had contacted** us.*

✗ *We would have appreciated it if you ~~would have~~ contacted us.*

**Circle the correct options.**

1 If I *would have to* / *had to* choose between the cakes, I would choose the strawberry one.

2 We *would have liked* / *'d like* to visit the palace, but we didn't have the chance.

3 It would have been better if there *would have been* / *had been* more jobs available.

4 The food wasn't as tasty as I *would have liked* / *'d like*.

5 If I'd known about the risks, I *wouldn't have taken* / *wouldn't take* part in the race.

6 My class could have learned more if the facilities *would have been* / *had been* better.

# VOCABULARY
## Being honest

→ SB p.40

**1** ★★☆ **Match the parts of the sentences.**

1 Why don't you just own ☐
2 If I tell a ☐
3 I can be very open ☐
4 It's always best to tell ☐
5 It isn't always easy to do ☐
6 There's no point hiding the ☐
7 My sister believed me – I never thought I'd get ☐
8 Dylan's always trying to cheat ☐

a with my mum – we have a great relationship.
b truth – people always find out in the end.
c lie, my face just goes bright red.
d away with that lie.
e in exams – he tries to look at my paper.
f the right thing, so thank you for being honest.
g up and tell her you broke her phone?
h the truth because then people will trust you.

**2** ★★☆ **Complete the dialogue with the words in the list. There is one extra word.**

do | get | hide | lie | open | own | truth

**Moira** So what do you think we should do? ¹_____ up and tell the ²_____ ?

**Rebecca** No way. She'll be furious. I think we have to tell a ³_____ and say it wasn't us.

**Moira** We'll never ⁴_____ away with it. I think we have to ⁵_____ the right thing.

**Rebecca** Which is?

**Moira** Be ⁶_____ about it. Say we were hungry and there was nothing else to eat.

**Rebecca** But it was her birthday cake! She won't accept that as an excuse.

**Moira** So what do you think we should do?

**Rebecca** ⁷_____ the truth. Say the dog ate it.

**Moira** The dog? That's brilliant! Why didn't we think of that before?

## Making a decision

→ SB p.43

**3** ★★☆ **Match the phrases (1–6) with the definitions (a–f).**

1 first thought ☐
2 to think long and hard ☐
3 to change your mind ☐
4 to reconsider ☐
5 to make up your mind ☐
6 the wrong decision ☐

a to really consider something
b to think about your decision again
c to come to a decision
d not the right decision
e to come to a different decision
f original idea

**4** ★★★ **Answer these questions so they're true for you.**

1 What were your first thoughts when you met your best friend?
_____

2 What is the best decision you have ever made?
_____

3 When was the last time you made the wrong decision about something?
_____

4 When is it difficult to make up your mind?
_____

5 Can you remember when you changed your mind about something? What was it?
_____

6 What kind of things do you have to think long and hard about?
_____

## WordWise: Phrases with *now*

→ SB p.43

**5** ★★☆ **Rewrite the sentences so that they have *now* in the correct place.**

1 I go out dancing with my friends and again, but I'm not very keen.
_____

2 Zac left just, so if you run, you'll catch him.
_____

3 We hardly ever see Jason that he's got his own scooter.
_____

4 We've missed the last bus. What are we going to do?
_____

# REFERENCE

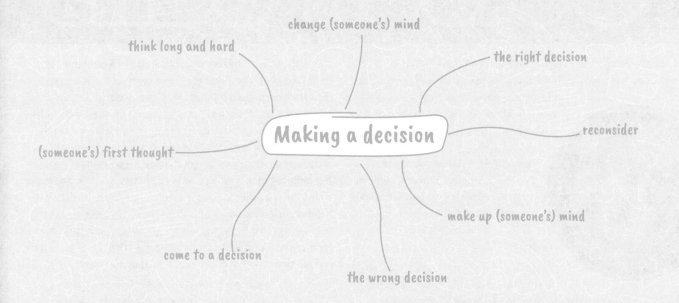

think long and hard

change (someone's) mind

the right decision

**Making a decision**

reconsider

(someone's) first thought

make up (someone's) mind

come to a decision

the wrong decision

## BEING HONEST

| bad | good |
|-----|------|
| cheat | be open about (something) |
| get away with (something) | do the right thing |
| hide the truth | own up (to something) |
| tell a lie | tell the truth |

## PHRASES WITH *NOW*

| now (= at this moment) | now (= in the near future) |
|------------------------|----------------------------|
| now and again | just now |
| now that | |

# VOCABULARY *EXTRA*

**1** **Match the phrases (1–6) with the sentences (a–f).**

1 take something seriously ☐
2 take someone's word for it ☐
3 keep a secret ☐
4 owe someone an apology ☐
5 as a matter of fact ☐
6 as far as I know ☐

a Nobody else must know.
b This is actually true.
c I believe what she says.
d I believe this is true.
e Pay attention – this is important.
f I made a mistake – I should say sorry.

**2** **Complete the dialogue.**

> a matter | an apology | far as
> take me | to keep | your word

**A** You didn't ¹_____ seriously! You told Kate about the surprise.
**B** As ²_____ of fact, she already knew about it.
**A** That doesn't matter. You owe me ³_____ .
**B** Sorry. As ⁴_____ I know, she doesn't know what the surprise is.
**A** OK, but she knows there is a surprise. You promised ⁵_____ the secret and I took ⁶_____ for it!

**3** **Rewrite the sentences with the phrases in Exercise 1.**

1 My friend told me not to tell anyone her news.
_____

2 I'm sorry I took my brother's camera without asking.
_____

3 I know what my friend tells me is always true.
_____

4 We should all realise that climate change is a serious problem.
_____

# Golden balls

A few years ago, there was a game show on TV in which the contestants faced a really difficult dilemma. I can't really remember what happened in the show. I just remember how it finished. ¹At the end, there were two contestants and they had the chance to win some money. Depending on how successful they'd been during the show, the amount of money could be anything from a few hundred pounds to over £50,000. To get their hands on this money, they had to make one final decision.

In front of each of them were two balls. One had the word 'split' inside, the other had the word 'steal'. ²If they wanted to share the money, they chose the 'split' ball. If they wanted to keep all the money for themselves, they chose the 'steal' ball. Each player chose a ball and then they showed it to each other at exactly the same time.

But it wasn't quite so simple. If they both chose the 'split' ball, then each contestant went home with half the money. If one player chose 'split' while the other chose 'steal', then the one who'd stolen won all the money, leaving the other player with nothing at all. However, if they both chose 'steal', then neither of them got any money.

Before they chose the ball, both players had a few minutes to explain to each other what they were going to do. Of course, they always promised they'd share, but they weren't always telling the truth. It wasn't cheating because those were the rules of the game. I remember always feeling really pleased when the two players kept their promises and they both won some of the prize money. ³It's always good to see the best side of people. But unfortunately, it didn't always end that way. When one player stole from the other, it made me feel really bad, especially when there was a large amount of cash involved. ⁴However, I think the best feeling I had was when two greedy players both stole. It was great to see the look of disappointment on their faces when they realised they'd both thrown away a great opportunity.

The programme showed all sides of human nature: the good and the ugly. As a matter of fact, social scientists watched it – for work, not fun! – to understand how contestants made up their minds to 'split' or 'steal'. On average, about half of the contestants were happy to share the prize. The main issues when deciding were the size of the prize and trust (for example, if the other player had lied in the earlier part of the game). As far as I know, ⁵the show only lasted a few years before they stopped making it. I think that was probably the right thing to do.

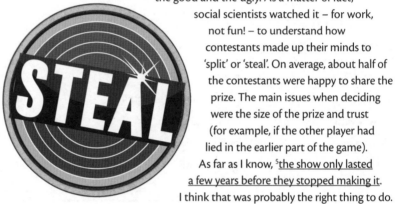

## READING

**1** **Read the article. What was the dilemma the game show contestants faced?**

_____

**2** **Read the text again. Mark the sentences T (true) or F (false). Then correct the false sentences.**

1 If contestants played well in the first part of the show, the prize money would increase. ☐

2 Each player kept the word in their ball secret from the other player. ☐

3 Both players won some money in the end. ☐

4 The best result for the writer was when both players 'split'. ☐

5 There were often social scientists among the contestants on the show. ☐

**3** **Read the article again and answer the questions.**

There are two players, Emily and Jordan. There is a total prize money of £10,000.

How much does each player win in the situations below? How does the writer feel watching it?

1 They both choose the 'split' ball.
   Emily £_____    Jordan £_____    Writer feels _____

2 They both choose the 'steal' ball.
   Emily £_____    Jordan £_____    Writer feels _____

3 Jordan chooses 'split', Emily chooses 'steal'.
   Emily £_____    Jordan £_____    Writer feels _____

4 Jordan chooses 'steal', Emily chooses 'split'.
   Emily £_____    Jordan £_____    Writer feels _____

**4** **CRITICAL THINKING** **Read the underlined parts of the article. Decide if they express a fact (F) or an opinion (O).**

1 _____     3 _____     5 _____
2 _____     4 _____

**5** **Imagine you are a contestant in the show. There is a prize of £10,000. What would you do and why? Write a short paragraph.**

# DEVELOPING *Writing*

## A diary entry about a dilemma

1 **INPUT** Read Zara's diary entry. What is her dilemma and what does she decide to do?

_____

### DIARY

I haven't shown my best friend, Nell, the trust she deserves and I'm feeling really bad about it. It all started when she asked to borrow my phone to check her social-media messages. Of course, I let her use it. (A) The problem is that she forgot to log out of her account afterwards, so when I used it a few hours later, her messages were the first things I saw. I was just about to log into my account when I noticed a message with my name in the subject line. (B) There it was – a message from my brother to my best friend with my name in the first line! Why was my name there? Why were they writing about me? I thought ¹_____ . I knew I should just close the page, but I couldn't help reading it. I knew it was the ²_____ to make but I opened the message. (C) As soon as I read it, I realised I'd made a horrible mistake. The message was all about arranging a surprise party for my birthday next week.

Now I've got a horrible dilemma. Should I ³_____ and ⁴_____ or say nothing and ⁵_____ from her? If I was braver, I'd tell her what I'd done. (D) I think that this time I won't say anything and pretend that the party is a surprise. But I know one thing – I'll never let anyone use my phone to check their messages again!

2 Complete the diary entry with the phrases in the list. There is one extra phrase you won't need.

hide the truth | long and hard | own up | tell a lie | tell her the truth | wrong decision

3 **ANALYSE** Complete the sentences with the correct form of the verbs in brackets to make second or third conditionals. Then decide in which of the spaces (A–D) they go.

1 If I _____ (can turn) back time, I _____ (close) the page without taking a look. ☐

2 If I _____ (not see) it, I _____ (never think) of reading any of her messages. ☐

3 If I _____ (tell) her, she _____ (never speak) to me again. ☐

4 If I _____ just _____ (say) no, I _____ (not have) this dilemma. ☐

4 Read the dilemmas. Then complete the conditional sentences.

1 I broke my brother's games console.
   a If I'd been more careful,
   _____ .
   b If he knew it was me,
   _____ .

2 I saw my classmate cheating in an exam.
   a If I told the teacher,
   _____ .
   b If she had studied harder,
   _____ .

3 My friend wants to borrow £100 from me. It's all the money I've got.
   a If I gave it to him and he never paid me back, _____ .
   b If he had been more careful with his money, _____ .

5 **PLAN** Choose one of the dilemmas in Exercise 4 or think of one of your own. Then make a plan for your diary entry.

• explain the dilemma
• describe how it happened
• say what you should and shouldn't have done
• say what you have learned from the experience

6 **PRODUCE** Write a diary entry about your dilemma (250 words). Use your notes from Exercise 5. Make sure you include all the points in the checklist.

## ✔ CHECKLIST

Use informal language.
Imagine what would happen using second conditional sentences.
Imagine what would have happened using third conditional sentences.
Use some of the phrases about being honest and making decisions from page 39.

# LISTENING

1 🔊 4.01 **Listen to three dialogues. Match them with the pictures.**

2 🔊 4.01 **Listen again and match the sentences with the dialogues. There is one extra sentence.**

Dialogue 1 ☐
Dialogue 2 ☐
Dialogue 3 ☐

a Someone did the right thing.
b Someone cheated.
c Someone told a lie.
d Someone made a mistake.

3 🔊 4.01 **Listen again and complete these parts of the dialogues.**

1
A ¹_____ . I was going to send a message, but I forgot.
B I hope you were careful with them.
A ²_____ . They're like new!

2
A Olivia, can you tell me what happened?
B I don't know what to say. ³_____ .
A Thank you for owning up and speaking for the class, Olivia.
B It was a stupid thing to do. ⁴_____ .

3
A If you had looked where you were going, this ⁵_____ !
B I'm sorry. ⁶_____ .

# DIALOGUE

4 **Put the dialogue in order.**

| 1 | Talia | Tell me it's not your birthday today. |
| ☐ | Talia | It isn't fine. I'm going straight out and getting you something nice. |
| ☐ | Talia | But I haven't got you a present or even a card. I feel awful about this. |
| ☐ | Talia | What are you doing? |
| ☐ | Talia | And tonight I'm taking you out for a meal. No argument. |
| 13 | Talia | Oh. I see. |
| ☐ | Talia | And I've forgotten it. I'm so embarrassed. |
| ☐ | Lena | Don't be so silly. It's easily done. |
| ☐ | Lena | No seriously. You don't need to. |
| ☐ | Lena | It is. It's the big one – 18. |
| ☐ | Lena | No worries. It's fine. |
| ☐ | Lena | But I can't. I've kind of got plans already. |
| ☐ | Lena | Well, it's just me and a few friends going out dancing. |

# PHRASES FOR FLUENCY    → SB p.44

5 **Complete the phrases with the missing vowels.**

1 _r_ y__ __t _f y__r m_nd?
2 b_l__v_ _t _r n_t ...
3 b_tw__n y__ _nd m_ ...
4 _ w_s w_nd_r_ng _f ...
5 _ny ch_nc_ ...?
6 wh_t's w_th ...?

6 **Complete the dialogues with the phrases from Exercise 5.**

1 A _____ the grumpy face, Brendan? Life isn't so bad, is it?
   B No, I'm just a bit tired. I didn't get a lot of sleep last night.

2 A I think we should take a break and go and play some tennis.
   B _____ , I was thinking exactly the same thing!

3 A Um, Jenni, I don't know if you're busy tonight but _____ you'd like to go to the cinema with me?
   B Like to? I'd love to!

4 A We've got visitors and the living room's a mess. It needs tidying – Thomas, _____ of doing that?
   B Sorry, Mum, but I'm busy playing Minecraft.

5 A That cat's really cute. I think we should take it home with us.
   B _____ It probably belongs to someone.

6 A Are you going to Yolanda's party?
   B _____ , I don't really want to go so I think I might make up an excuse and give it a miss.

## PRONUNCIATION
Consonant–vowel word linking
Go to page 119. 🎧

## WRITING
*A story*

### EXAM GUIDE

**For this task, there is a choice of four questions. You have to choose <u>one</u> question to answer. The text types include: an article, a review, an essay, an email or letter or a story.**

- Before you start writing, think about what you want to write and make a brief plan.
- Organise your text into clear paragraphs and use linkers to connect ideas and show the sequence of events.
- Make sure you start with a brief introduction, and end with a conclusion.
- Use formal, informal or neutral language, according to the type of text you choose.
- Try to use a range of grammatical structures, vocabulary and verb forms.
- Keep within the word limit and remember that you have about 40 minutes for each of the texts.

**1** Look at the task. <u>Underline</u> the most important information in it.

**WE ARE LOOKING FOR STORIES FOR A NEW WEBSITE FOR TEENAGERS.**

Your story must start with the following sentence:

*I opened the suitcase and could hardly believe my eyes – it was more money than I had ever seen in my life.*

Your story must include:
- a decision
- a police officer.

Write your story in 140–190 words.

**2** Read Nico's answer. Which part of the question does he fail to answer?

I opened the suitcase and could hardly believe my eyes – it was more money than I had ever seen in my life. I closed it quickly and put the case back onto the seat. I was excited, but I was also very nervous. I sat down and thought about how this case had fallen into my hands.

The woman had seemed normal. We'd started chatting, first about the weather and then about where we were going. She was on her way to visit her aunt. When a man in a dark suit passed by, her mood suddenly changed. She seemed anxious and didn't want to talk. Then she got up and asked me to look after the case and left. Two hours later, the train had reached the station where I was getting off. What was I going to do? Leave the money on the train or take it with me?

I counted the money when I got home: £100,000 exactly. I used it to open a small shop. Now, more than 20 years later, I have a chain of 50 stores across the country. I wonder who that woman was.

**3** Look at the notes Nico made before writing. Use his story to answer the questions he asked himself.

1 Where was I?

_____

2 Why did I have this suitcase?

_____

3 How did I feel when I saw the money?

_____

4 What did I decide to do?

_____

5 What were the consequences?

_____

**4** Read the task. Plan and then write your answer.

**WE ARE LOOKING FOR STORIES FOR AN ENGLISH LANGUAGE MAGAZINE FOR TEENAGERS.**

Your story must start with the following sentence:

*Should I stay or should I go? I had 30 seconds to decide.*

Your story must include:
- an animal
- a bike.

Write your story in 140–190 words.

**5** Ask a friend to read your story and complete the sentences about it.

I really like the ...

_____

I thought the story was ...

_____

The language you used was ...

_____

You could improve it by ...

_____

# CONSOLIDATION

## 🎧 LISTENING

**1** 🔊 4.04 **Listen to the dialogue. Choose the correct answer (A, B or C).**

1 The girl doesn't want the T-shirt because …
   A it's too big.
   B she doesn't like the colour.
   C she doesn't like the name on it.

2 The girl wants to exchange the T-shirt for …
   A a belt.
   B a different T-shirt.
   C two other T-shirts.

3 The man suggests that the girl could …
   A keep the T-shirt.
   B give the T-shirt to her brother.
   C give the T-shirt to someone else.

**2** 🔊 4.04 **Listen again and mark the sentences T (true) or F (false).**

1 The girl doesn't like clothes with the names of companies on. ☐

2 All the clothes in the shop have the company name on. ☐

3 The T-shirt was a present from the girl's brother. ☐

4 The shirt has a hole in it. ☐

5 The girl hasn't got the receipt. ☐

6 The belt is more expensive than the T-shirt. ☐

7 The girl is bigger than her friend Jenny. ☐

8 She decides to give the T-shirt to her friend. ☐

## 🔤 VOCABULARY

**3** **Match the sentences.**

1 Everyone knows who she is. ☐
2 She's travelled all over the world. ☐
3 She's totally honest. ☐
4 She just doesn't know what to do. ☐
5 She stuck with her original decision. ☐
6 She doesn't want to use her real name. ☐

a She can't make up her mind at all.
b So she's decided to use a stage name.
c She didn't want to change her mind.
d She's a big name in this country.
e I've never heard her tell a lie.
f You name it, she's been there!

**4** Circle the correct options.

1 I haven't decided yet – I'm going to think long and *hard / strong* about it.

2 We don't go there very often – just *now that / now and again*.

3 Come on, tell us the *lie / truth* about what happened.

4 I know you did it. Come on, you should just *get away with it / own up to it*.

5 I really don't care if people *make me / call me* names.

6 I think you've made the wrong decision. If you want to *reconsider / come to a decision*, please call me.

7 I don't like the *logo / brand* of this company. It isn't very well designed.

8 He's the owner of a big *chain / brand* of shops in the north of the country.

## ⓖ GRAMMAR

**5** **Correct the sentences.**

1 I wish you are here.
   _____

2 I was happier if the weather was better.
   _____

3 If only I know the answer to this question.
   _____

4 We'd better to leave now, I think.
   _____

5 I'll phone you when I'll get home.
   _____

6 Do you think we should asking for some help?
   _____

7 He's a great guitar player – if only he can sing better.
   _____

8 If he'd left earlier, he hadn't missed the start of the film.
   _____

9 The bus ride there is free, so you have to pay for it.
   _____

10 Let's wait as soon as 5 pm to call them.
   _____

## DIALOGUE

**6** 🔊 **4.05** **Complete the dialogue with the phrases in the list. Then listen and check.**

> any chance | are you out of your mind
> believe it or not | between you and me
> had better | I was wondering
> should have been | what's with

**Maya** Hey, Jonah. ¹_____
if you're going to Laura's party later.

**Jonah** Yeah, I'm going. Why?

**Maya** ²_____ I can go with
you? I just don't like arriving at
parties on my own.

**Jonah** Sure, no problem.

**Maya** That's great. Thanks. Hey, you'll
never guess what happened to me
in a shop this morning.

**Jonah** Tell me. What happened?

**Maya** Well, I bought a really cool
shirt for the party tonight.
³_____ , it was
£79.99! I can't believe I spent so
much!

**Jonah** Wow, that's really expensive.
But, so what?

**Maya** Well, you know, my parents gave
me some money for my birthday,
so I paid cash with two £50 notes.
I put them on the counter, and,
⁴_____ , the woman
put the change on top of the notes!
I picked it all up and left. So, I got
the shirt and my money and the
change! How cool is that?

**Jonah** Cool? ⁵_____ ?
It's dishonest. Think about the poor
shop assistant – she'll probably have
to pay that money out of her own
pocket. You ⁶_____
take it back and explain. Say it was
a mistake.

**Maya** No way. She ⁷_____
more careful.

**Jonah** Whatever. I'm sure you wouldn't
like it to happen to you.

**Maya** Oh, come on, Jonah.
⁸_____ you?
Don't be so boring.

**Jonah** Boring? Maya, what you did
was stealing, you know?

## READING

This week, I've been looking at bags – school
bags and sports bags for your PE kit. There's
a huge choice out there, so I've done the hard
work and picked the best ones for you all.

**BACKPACK:** NORTHPACK 'COLLEGE': £30

**GOOD:** If you like backpacks, you must try this! It's available in ten
colours – so there ought to be a colour you like! It doesn't look very big,
but it's surprising how much you can fit in it. There's a special secure
pocket for your laptop and two more pockets for books.

**BUT:** I wish it had an extra pocket because I have to carry loads of books.

**MY CHOICE:** because it's so comfortable to carry. If you get backache,
I'd definitely recommend this backpack.

**MESSENGER BAG:** COURIER 'DAILY' SPECIAL PRICE: £28

**GOOD:** Stylish, well-made bag from a top brand. It's specially designed
for students, so there's plenty of space for everything. You don't have to
worry about your things getting wet because it's waterproof.

**BUT:** If only there was a small pocket on the outside for a phone …

**MY CHOICE:** because I love the design and the special price. If it hadn't
been on special offer, it would have cost £40!

**SPORTS BAG:** EACTIVE 'TOP KIT': £15

**GOOD:** This is a well-designed sports bag and ideal for your school PE kit.
It's strong and it's got a special space for shoes, so you don't have to put
them in a separate bag.

**BUT:** I wish it was a brighter colour … but if it was a light colour,
it wouldn't stay clean for long!

**MY CHOICE:** because it's light and excellent value for money. You
wouldn't find this quality at a lower price!

**7** **Read the blog and answer the questions.**

1 What is the purpose of the blog?
_____

2 What would Suzie like to change about the backpack?
_____

3 How much can you save on the price of the messenger bag?
_____

4 What does Suzie think about the quality of the sports bag?
_____

5 What would be the disadvantage of a light colour sports bag?
_____
_____

## ✏️ WRITING

**8** **Think of two products you know: one that you like the name
of, and one that you don't like the name of. Write a short text
(150–200 words). Include information about:**

- what the products are and what they do
- what their names are and why you like/dislike the names.

# 5 STORYTELLING

Grammar rap! ▶13

## GRAMMAR
### Relative pronouns
→ SB p.50

1 ★☆☆ **Complete the sentences with *who, whose, where* or *which*.**

1 The book _____ I have just read is called *Clockwork Angel*.

2 It is a fantasy novel _____ was written by Cassandra Clare.

3 The name of the girl _____ is the heroine of the novel is Tessa Gray.

4 The story is set in London, _____ all the action takes place.

5 Tessa Gray is looking for her brother, _____ has disappeared.

6 Tessa gets help from two friends _____ names are Will and Jem.

### Defining and non-defining relative clauses
→ SB p.50

2 ★★☆ **Combine the sentences about a famous vampire with *who, which, where* or *whose*.**

0 Abhartach was a vampire. He came from Ireland.
*Abhartach was a vampire who came from Ireland.*

1 It was a legend. It inspired Bram Stoker to write *Dracula*.
_____
_____

2 Abhartach was an evil magician. He had very strong powers.
_____
_____

3 He lived in Derry. He ruled a small kingdom.
_____
_____

4 He was an evil ruler. His people were afraid of him.
_____
_____

5 *Dracula* comes from an Irish word. It means 'bad blood'.
_____
_____

3 ★★☆ **Complete the dialogue with *which, who, that, where* or *whose*.**

**Ella** What kind of books do you like reading?

**Beth** I like reading books ¹_____ are set in the olden days. My favourite book is one about a girl ²_____ grandmother lives in a very old house. It's a fantasy novel about the people ³_____ used to live in the house.

**Ella** Is it set in England?

**Beth** No, it's set in the US, ⁴_____ Maryanne, the girl, is sent to spend the summer holidays with her grandmother. What about you? What kind of books do you like?

**Ella** I like historical novels. I'm reading one now ⁵_____ is set in Victorian England. It's about a poor girl ⁶_____ has to work. She works for a doctor ⁷_____ main job is to look after his patients, but he's also a scientist. The girl helps him with his experiments.

**Beth** It sounds like the kind of book ⁸_____ I'd like to read. Can I borrow it when you've finished?

4 ★★☆ **Put the words in order to make sentences with non-defining relative clauses.**

1 aunt, / My / lives / in / Berlin, / who / an / author / is
_____
_____

2 film, / The / stars / Lucy Heyton, / which / out / in / cinemas / is / now
_____
_____

3 storyteller, / The / work / all / over / the / world, / whose / takes / him / in / Japan / is / at / moment / the
_____
_____

4 Prague, / where / boy / the / story / the / in / grew up, / my / hometown / is
_____
_____

5 heroine / story, / the / of / The / whose / father / French, / is / called / Sophie / is
_____
_____

**5** ★★☆ **Mark the relative clauses D (defining) or ND (non-defining).**

1 My favourite book, which is about a moon landing, has now been made into a film. ____

2 Leo, who had already read the book, liked the film. ____

3 The man who she's interviewing wrote the book. ____

4 I couldn't find any travel books on Morocco, where I'm going on holiday next month. ____

5 My aunt, who is a poet, lives in London. ____

6 The girl whose father was rescued in the story was Spanish. ____

7 The fairy story, which was written in the 19th century, is still read today. ____

8 I couldn't watch the horror film which was on TV last night. ____

**6** ★★★ **Rewrite the sentences with who, which, where or whose and the clauses in brackets.**

0 The girl had long red hair. (mother is the heroine of the story)
   *The girl, whose mother is the heroine of the story, had long red hair.*

1 The city is my hometown. (all the action took place)
   _____
   _____

2 The park is the scene of the crime. (the stolen documents were found)
   _____
   _____

3 The story is very sad. (is set in a future world)
   _____
   _____

4 The villain was in fact a good man. (disappeared at the end of the story)
   _____
   _____

5 The meeting was the start of the adventure. (took place in a forest)
   _____
   _____

## Relative clauses with which   → SB p.53

**7** ★★☆ **Read the sentence pairs. Write a new (third) sentence so that it has the same meaning as the sentence pair. Use which.**

0 My parents used to read lots of stories to me when I was a child. I enjoyed this a lot.
   *My parents used to read lots of stories to me when I was a child, which I enjoyed a lot.*

1 Their train arrived four hours late. This meant they missed the show.
   _____

2 None of the students had studied for the test. This made the teacher really angry.
   _____

3 My friend Lia reads ten books a month. I find this amazing.
   _____

4 Most of my friends don't like the new Avengers film. I can't understand this.
   _____

**8** ★★★ **Complete the sentences so that they are true for you.**

1 One of my friends _____ , which is very good news.

2 Lots of people in my street _____ , which I find annoying.

3 Not many people want to _____ , which I find a great pity.

## GET IT RIGHT!

**that vs. which in relative clauses**

Learners sometimes mistakenly use **that** in non-defining relative clauses.

We can use **which** or **that** in defining relative clauses.

✓ This is the solution **that** you are looking for.
✓ This is the solution **which** you are looking for.

We only use **which** in non-defining relative clauses.

✓ I'm in Brazil, **which** is a beautiful country.
✗ I'm in Brazil, **that** is a beautiful country.

Tick (✓) the sentences which can use **that** or **which**.
Cross (✗) the sentences where only **which** is possible.

1 Jade spent £100 on accessories, (which / that) is too much. ☐

2 I'd love to have a sports car (which / that) can go fast. ☐

3 Pete has a very old computer (which / that) has one of the first video games on it. ☐

4 We should buy the one (which / that) is cheaper. ☐

5 I won't be there, (which / that) is a problem. ☐

 **VOCABULARY**
Elements of a story  → SB p.51

1 ★★☆ **Complete the dialogue.**

> characters | ending | hero
> setting | plot | villain

**Josh** OK, ask me questions and try to guess the book I'm thinking of.

**Micky** Right. Where does the action take place?

**Josh** The [1]_____ for the story is an island, a few hundred years ago.

**Micky** What's it about?

**Josh** The [2]_____ is about a man whose ship was destroyed in a storm. He was the only person who survived and it's about his experiences on the desert island. The [3]_____ of the book is this man.
There aren't many other [4]_____ in the story because the man thinks he's alone on the island until one day when he meets a young man who also lives there.

**Micky** Who's the bad character then? Who's the [5]_____ ?

**Josh** There isn't one.

**Micky** And does it have a happy [6]_____ ?

**Josh** Yes, it does.

**Micky** I think it's *Robinson Crusoe* by Daniel Defoe.

**Josh** Well guessed! You're right. Now your turn.

2 ★★★ **Use the words in Exercise 1 to complete this dialogue about a story (or a film) that you like.**

**Micky** Where does the action take place?

**Me** The _____ for the story is _____ .

**Micky** What's it about?

**Me** The _____ .

**Micky** Who is the hero or heroine of the book?

**Me** _____ .

**Micky** Who's the bad character then? Who's the _____ ?

**Me** _____ .

**Micky** And does it have a happy _____ ?

**Me** _____ .

**Micky** I think it's _____ by _____ .

3 ★★☆ **Complete the sentences with the words in the list.**

> blockbuster | influential | tradition
> romance | anecdotes | special effects

1 Nelson Mandela's _____ book *A Long Walk to Freedom* made people aware of the inequalities between people.

2 The two main characters fall in love, and the film follows their _____ .

3 My friend tells lots of funny _____ about her family.

4 The novel, which was very successful, was made into a _____ film.

5 It was a science fiction story, so the film had lots of amazing _____ .

6 Our family has a _____ of telling stories on Christmas Day.

## Types of story
→ SB p.53

4 ★☆☆ **Match the book descriptions (a–g) with the genres (1–7).**

1 horror story ☐
2 (auto)biography ☐
3 romantic novel ☐
4 historical novel ☐
5 crime novel ☐
6 science fiction novel ☐
7 fantasy novel ☐

a *War Horse* by Michael Morpurgo is set during the First World War. Albert's father sells his horse Joey to the army and he goes into battle in France.

b In *Noughts and Crosses* by Malorie Blackman, Sephy is a cross and Callum is a nought. They fall in love, but in their world, noughts and crosses shouldn't be friends. Like Romeo and Juliet, their love is forbidden.

c *Frankenstein* by Mary Shelley, which was published in 1818, is often considered to be the first book of its genre. It's the story about how a strange creature was created by a scientist.

d *Northern Lights* by Philip Pullman is the first of three stories about Lyra's journey through different worlds. Everyone in the story has an animal which represents their personality.

e *Haunted* by R. L. Stine is about a girl who is visited by a ghost from the future. Together they try to stop the death of a boy from happening. Sometimes it's quite scary.

f *The London Eye Mystery* by Siobhan Dowd. Ted and Kat's cousin Salim gets on the London Eye. He never gets off again. Ted and Kat follow the clues across London to help the police to find their cousin.

g *Boy: Tales of Childhood* by Roald Dahl is about the author's childhood in Wales and his time at an English boarding school.

# REFERENCE

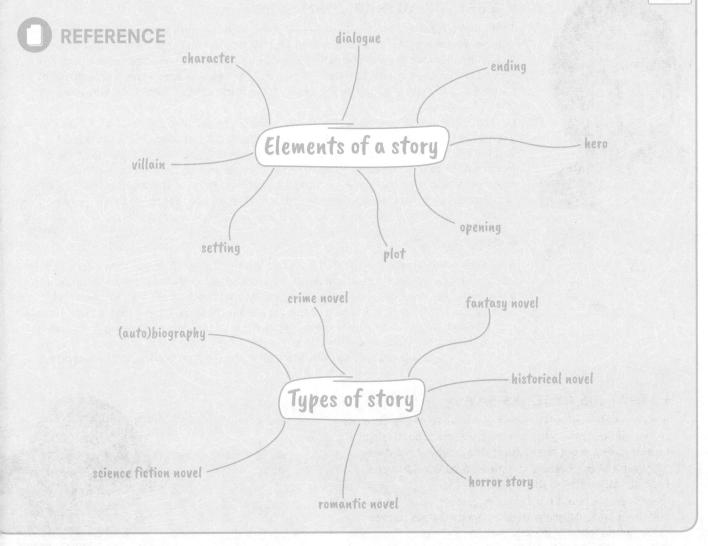

Elements of a story

- dialogue
- character
- ending
- hero
- villain
- setting
- plot
- opening

Types of story

- crime novel
- fantasy novel
- (auto)biography
- historical novel
- science fiction novel
- horror story
- romantic novel

# VOCABULARY *EXTRA*

**1  Complete the mind map.**

chapter | essay | poetry | scene
short story | travel literature

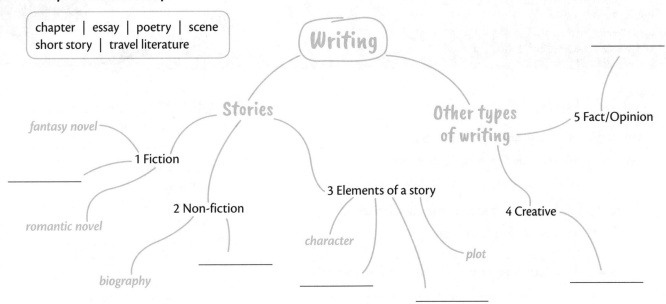

Writing

Stories

Other types of writing

5 Fact/Opinion

fantasy novel

1 Fiction

_____

romantic novel

2 Non-fiction

3 Elements of a story

4 Creative

character

plot

biography

_____

_____

_____

_____

**2  Write an example that you know of each genre.**

1  short story: _____

2  poetry: _____

3  travel literature: _____

**3  Complete the sentences with your own ideas.**

1  The last essay I wrote was about _____ .

2  In my favourite book, the best scene is when _____ .

3  I prefer books with *long* / *short* / *no* chapters because _____ .

## ▶ MEET THE AUTHOR: JOHN GREEN

Today we're reading about … John Green! John, who is American, is one of the top authors of teenage literature in the world today. He's already won several book prizes and has a huge number of fans. Over 45 million of his print books have been sold worldwide and his stories have been translated into as many as 54 languages. Have you read any of his books? You might have seen *The Fault in Our Stars* (2014), which is the film version of one of his novels.

But that's not all! Oh, no! He is also well known for the online content which he creates and presents with his brother, Hank. *VlogBrothers*, which has been online since 2007, was their first YouTube channel. They post videos every week on a wide range of topics from comedy to serious world issues. They encourage their subscribers to join their community, and they are always creating new projects to bring teenagers together. *Crash Course*, which they started in 2011, is an educational channel whose aim is to teach topics in a way that is enjoyable and easy to understand.

## ▶ BIOGRAPHY

John Green was born in Indiana, but has lived in a number of different towns across the US. After studying Literature at university, he worked as a book reviewer in Chicago for a few years. His first book, *Looking for Alaska*, was published in 2005 and immediately won a prize for the best teen novel of the year. It is a romance set in a high school. He says that he was trying to remember his own experiences of bullying and feeling lonely while he was writing the story. Since then, he has written more novels and collections of short stories. He now combines writing with the online projects that he does with his brother.

## ▶ WHAT HIS READERS SAY

'His books are well written, his style is easy-going and he uses words that people my age use. At the same time, though, he also writes about world issues. That's why I love them.'

'I enjoy his books because the stories are believable and I can identify with the characters.'

'His novels are about normal young people – like me and my friends. People with good and bad sides to their personality. Nobody's perfect.'

'When I start a John Green book, I can't put it down until I've finished it! The story becomes part of my life. He's the best!'

'He understands what it's like to be young today. His stories are like real life and he writes how teenagers think.'

'John Green knows his readers are intelligent and that we can understand difficult stuff.'

## 📖 READING

1 **Read the article and answer the question.**

What two things is John Green well known for?

_____

2 **Read the article again and answer the questions.**

1 What kind of books does John Green write?

_____

2 How does he encourage teenagers to interact with each other?

_____

3 How successful was his first book? How do you know?

_____

4 What do readers say about the way he writes?

_____

5 What do readers like about the characters in his books?

_____

3 CRITICAL THINKING **Put the events from John Green's life in chronological order.**

- [ ] a A film of one of his books came out.
- [ ] b He began making videos to help students.
- [ ] c He had a bad time with people of his own age.
- [ ] d He published his first novel.
- [1] e He was born in Indiana, US.
- [ ] f He started working with his brother.
- [ ] g He wrote book reviews.
- [ ] h He went to university.

4 **Who is your favourite author? Write a short text to introduce the author and say why you like him/her.**

# DEVELOPING *Writing*

## A book review

1  **INPUT**  **Look at the book cover and choose the genre you think it is. Then read the review and check.**

☐ horror story ☐ travel literature ☐ crime novel ☐ science fiction

**1** *The Boy Who Biked the World* is a travel adventure. It was written by Alastair Humphreys, who completed a four-year bicycle ride around the world. In the story, the hero is a boy called Tom, who really wants to be an explorer. His favourite book is an atlas and he is more interested in adventurers than he is in footballers. One day, Tom finally sets off on his own adventure. He travels through Europe, the Middle East and Africa on his bicycle. The story is full of fascinating facts about the countries he travelled through, and the characters he meets.

**2** One of my favourite parts was the opening of the book. Tom is caught daydreaming in his Maths class, which has happened to me, too. I loved Tom. My favourite thing about the book, however, was the funny illustrations and amusing little notes.

**3** I would definitely recommend this book to anyone who loves geography and wants to go on an adventure. Although the book is for 8- to 12-year-olds, I think older kids will enjoy reading it, too, and it's perfect for students learning English. I give this book 4 out of 5 stars because it's very interesting.

THE BOY WHO BIKED THE WORLD

ALASTAIR HUMPHREYS
ILLUSTRATED BY TOM MORGAN-JONES

★★★★☆

2  **ANALYSE**  **Read the review again and answer the questions.**

Paragraph 1
1  What is the story about?
_____
_____

2  Where does the story take place?
_____

Paragraph 2
3  What happened to the main character that the writer of the review can identify with?
_____
_____

4  Did the writer of the review like the book? What was his/her favourite thing about it?
_____

Paragraph 3
5  Which age group does the writer of the review recommend the book for?
_____

6  How does the writer of the review rate the book? What are his/her reasons?
_____

3  **Match the paragraphs (1–3) with the content (a–c).**

Paragraph 1 ☐    Paragraph 2 ☐    Paragraph 3 ☐

a  overall opinion and recommendations
b  factual information and short summary of the plot
c  the parts the reviewer enjoyed most

4  **Match the parts of the sentences.**

1  The **hero** or **heroine** of the book ☐
2  The **setting** ☐
3  The **opening sentence** ☐
4  It is very important to have a strong **ending** ☐
5  Some authors include jokes and amusing **dialogue** ☐
6  There may be several **characters** ☐

a  should catch the reader's attention.
b  which makes the story more entertaining.
c  which satisfies the reader.
d  is usually is the main character.
e  is where the action takes place.
f  who have different strong and weak points.

5  **PLAN**  **Choose a book to review. Answer the questions in Exercise 2 about your book. Then use your answers to plan paragraphs, as in Exercise 3.**

6  **PRODUCE**  **Write your book review (200–250 words). Use your plan from Exercise 5. Make sure you include all the points in the checklist.**

✓ **CHECKLIST**

Arrange your ideas in paragraphs.
Use some adjectives to make your review more interesting.
Use long sentences with *which, who, whose* and *where*.

# 🎧 LISTENING

**1** 🔊 5.01  **Read the sentences. Then listen and write the numbers of the conversations (1, 2 or 3).**

a  He sees three footballers who play for his favourite football team.  ☐

b  She sees a famous actor whose name she has forgotten.  ☐

c  She sees a friend of a friend that she hasn't seen for months.  ☐

d  He was in a restaurant, where he was having a meal with his parents.  ☐

e  She was in a shop, where she was choosing a book.  ☐

f  She was shopping on Oxford Street.  ☐

**2** 🔊 5.01  **Listen again and mark the sentences T (true) or F (false).**

1  Katie saw her best friend in the bookshop.  ☐

2  Sometimes Amanda thinks about somebody and then they phone or text her.  ☐

3  Jake's team won the football match on Saturday.  ☐

4  Jake saw three Manchester United footballers in a restaurant.  ☐

5  Sarah was shopping in Oxford Street when she saw the famous actor.  ☐

6  The annoying thing was that Sarah can't remember the actor's address.  ☐

## DIALOGUE

**3** **Put the words in order to make sentences.**

1  never / what / believe / You'll / happened

_____ ?

2  strangest / me / to / happened / thing / The

_____ .

3  me / finish / Let

_____ .

4  the / That / annoying / thing / was

_____ .

5  the / are / chances / What

_____ ?

**4** **Put the dialogue in order.**

☐ **Matt**  Well, I haven't seen her for ages, but yesterday I was thinking about her – and then this morning I saw her. What are the chances, eh?

☐ **Matt**  Yes. And that's the annoying thing – you're always right!

☐ **Matt**  The strangest thing happened to me this morning. I saw that girl Josie in town!

☐ **Matt**  Yes, she does, but …

☐ **Iris**  Let me finish. And she works in a shop in town, too. So, it isn't strange at all. Am I right?

☐ **Iris**  You saw Josie? What's so strange about that?

☐ **Iris**  The chances are really good, actually. I mean, she lives here, doesn't she? And …

**5** **Complete the conversation with the words in the list. There is one extra word.**

> annoying | believe | chances
> finish | happened | strangest

**Lara**  You'll never ¹_____ what happened last night. That film *Scared* was on TV! It was just the ²_____ thing!

**Johnny**  Why? What's so strange about that? They show *Scared* a lot on TV.

**Lara**  Let me ³_____ . You see, I wanted to watch it on Sunday. I found the DVD at home, but the ⁴_____ thing was that it didn't work any more.

**Johnny**  Yes, I hate it when a DVD stops working properly.

**Lara**  But then the next day, I switched the TV on – and there it was! What are the ⁵_____ of that?

**Johnny**  That is a little strange.

PRONUNCIATION
The schwa /ə/ in word endings
Go to page 119. 🔊

# TOWARDS B2 First for Schools

 **READING AND USE OF ENGLISH**
*Multiple choice*

1 **You are going to read a review of Jules Verne's classic novel *Around the World in 80 Days*. For questions 1–3, choose the answer (A, B, C or D) which you think fits best according to the text.**

HOME | REVIEWS | LATEST NEWS | BLOG

## Around the World in 80 Days

Jules Verne's novel *Around the World in 80 Days* has encouraged many people to travel around the world in unusual ways. It has also inspired several films, TV series, theatre productions and even board and video games.

So, where did Jules Verne get the idea from? Jules Verne told a reporter that he had been sitting in a café in Paris one day when he saw a newspaper advertisement for the first ever tourist trip around the world in 1872.

In Jules Verne's story, a wealthy English gentleman, Phileas Fogg, accepts a bet of £20,000 that he can travel round the world in 80 days. Phileas Fogg is a man who is very hard to please. For example, he fires his servant because he brings him some water to wash himself in that is 29°C instead of 30°C. He has a very strict routine and he follows it to the letter every day.

Fogg employs a new servant, Passepartout, and on Wednesday, 2 October 1872, they set off on their journey round the world. While he's in India, Fogg falls in love with an Indian girl, Aouda. The journey ends back in London with Fogg believing that he has arrived a day too late and that he has lost the bet. He tells Aouda that he cannot marry her now, as he's too poor. Passepartout learns that they have got the date wrong. The party travelled eastward, so they gained a day. Fogg hurries to his club and arrives there just in time to win the bet, and the story ends happily.

The story is an easy read. The amusing twists and turns of the plot keep readers entertained throughout. It is a romantic adventure story that I would strongly recommend to all my friends.

1 What gave Jules Verne the idea for the story?
- A He was looking for an unusual sort of holiday.
- B He had heard about a ship that had sailed around the world.
- C A man in a café in Paris mentioned the idea to him.
- D He had read about a round-the-world holiday.

2 What does the reviewer mean by: 'he follows it to the letter'?
- A He writes letters about what he does.
- B He never changes the order of his daily habits.
- C He writes notes to remind his servant what to do.
- D He writes all his appointments in a diary.

3 What does Passepartout do to help Phileas Fogg win the bet?
- A He introduces Aouda to Phileas Fogg.
- B He notices that Fogg has made a mistake.
- C He manages to reach London before Fogg.
- D He helps Fogg cheat so that he arrives in time.

# 6 THAT'S IMPOSSIBLE!

## ⊙ GRAMMAR
### Present and past passive (review)  → SB p.58

**1** ★☆☆ (Circle) the correct options.

1 The best sports cars *make / are made* in Italy.

2 The concert *showed / was shown* live on TV.

3 Lorna *posts / is posted* all her photos on social media.

4 The 2016 Olympics *held / were held* in Rio de Janeiro.

5 My dad *makes / is made* model trains as a hobby.

6 Letters *deliver / aren't delivered* on Sundays.

7 Jacob's really good at tennis. He *coaches / is coached* by his mum.

8 A girl in my class *won / was won* the talent show.

**2** ★★☆ Complete the story with the past passive forms of the verbs in brackets.

The school magic show was a complete success. All the tickets ⁰ *were sold* (sell) and some amazing tricks ¹ _____ (perform) by three very talented magicians. Here are some of my favourites. The headmaster ² _____ (saw) in half. A piece of paper ³ _____ (turn) into hundreds of butterflies. Loads of gold coins ⁴ _____ (find) behind the ears of Adam from 6E. And of course, a rabbit ⁵ _____ (pull) out of a hat.

**3** ★★★ Make questions in the present or past passive using the prompts.

0 President Obama / elect
   *When was President Obama elected* ?

1 America / discover by Columbus
   When _____ ?

2 The first electric car / build
   When _____ ?

3 BMW cars / make
   Where _____ ?

4 The Glastonbury music festival / hold
   Where _____ ?

5 2018 FIFA World Cup final / play
   Where _____ ?

**4** ★★★ Write answers to the questions in Exercise 3. Use the clues in the list to help you.

> 1492 | 2004 | 2008 | England
> Germany | Moscow

0 *President Obama was elected in 2008.*

1 _____

2 _____

3 _____

4 _____

5 _____

### *have something done*  → SB p.59

**5** ★★☆ Read about the hotel, then complete the letter.

#### Welcome to the
## 👑 Ritz Carlton Hotel!
### We have everything you need for the perfect weekend.

0 We park your car on arrival.

1 We take your bags to your room.

2 A top chef cooks all your meals.

3 Room service brings your meals to your room.

4 We deliver tickets to top shows to your room.

5 We wash and iron all your clothes.

6 A top stylist cuts your hair for free.

We had a wonderful weekend at the Ritz hotel.

0 *We had our car parked for us when we arrived.*

1 _____

2 _____

3 _____

4 _____

5 _____

6 _____

**6** ⭐⭐⭐ **What did these people have done yesterday? Write sentences.**

**0** teeth / check
*He had his teeth*
*checked.*

**2** pizza / deliver
_____
_____

**1** hair / dye
_____
_____

**3** washing machine / fix
_____
_____

## Future and present perfect passive (review)

→ SB p.61

**7** ⭐☆☆ **Complete the blog post.**

> has been made | have been built
> haven't been painted | haven't been widened
> will be finished | will be put up
> will be shown | will be sold

🏠 HOME | ❓ ABOUT | 📰 NEWS | ✉ CONTACT

It's only six months until the Olympic Games open here, but is the city ready? All of the stadiums ¹_____ , but many of them ²_____ yet. The builders promise that they ³_____ before the opening day. The city airport
⁴_____ bigger to allow more planes to land here, but the roads from the airport into the city ⁵_____ and many people think the traffic will be a huge problem. Most of the tickets have been sold already and the organisers believe all of them
⁶_____ in the next few weeks.
So if you're planning to come, make sure you get yours soon. Big screens
⁷_____ around the city and many events ⁸_____ live on them, so even if you can't get into the stadiums, you can enjoy the amazing Olympic atmosphere in this beautiful city.

**8** ⭐⭐☆ **Complete the sentences with the present perfect passive form of the verbs in brackets.**

1 The windows are really dirty. They _____ (not clean) for months.
2 Have you heard the news? The bank robbers _____ (catch). They weren't happy!
3 The test _____ (mark). You can find out your score online.
4 We've been waiting for an hour and our food still _____ (not deliver).
5 Hey! Your bill _____ (not pay) yet.

**9** ⭐⭐⭐ **Rewrite the sentences using the passive.**

1 They'll play the final on Thursday.
_____
_____

2 They won't pay me until next month.
_____
_____

3 A famous actor will open the new shopping centre.
_____
_____

4 They've closed the hospital.
_____
_____

5 The earthquake has destroyed the whole city.
_____
_____

6 No one has seen the mountain climbers for days.
_____
_____

## GET IT RIGHT!

### Future passive

**Learners sometimes use the wrong tense where the future passive is needed, or use the future passive where it is not necessary.**

✓ The changes will be introduced next year.
✗ The changes will introduce next year.
✗ The changes are introduced next year.

**Correct the sentences.**

1 This money will use to develop the city.
_____

2 In the future the population will be increased.
_____

3 If the concert doesn't start soon, we are forced to leave.
_____

4 Please see the questionnaire which will be enclosed with this letter.
_____

5 The programme will show on Friday at 10 am.
_____

# VOCABULARY
## Extreme adjectives and modifiers

→ SB p.58

**1** ★☆☆ **Find ten extreme adjectives in the wordsearch. Then write them next to the non-extreme adjectives.**

| G | R | E | A | T | T | L | U | F | W | A |
|---|---|---|---|---|---|---|---|---|---|---|
| N | P | G | B | E | N | I | B | V | W | D |
| I | Y | A | Q | R | A | K | C | G | J | E |
| T | T | E | F | R | I | O | O | K | E | L |
| A | V | T | C | I | L | P | E | P | N | I |
| N | W | U | O | B | L | N | L | B | O | G |
| I | G | N | I | L | I | O | B | C | R | H |
| C | R | I | I | E | R | F | O | P | M | T |
| S | U | M | N | I | B | E | F | K | O | E |
| A | A | B | L | I | H | Y | T | F | U | D |
| F | A | N | T | A | S | T | I | C | S | D |

interesting ¹_____
happy ²_____
big ³_____
good (x3) ⁴_____ ,
⁵_____ , ⁶_____
bad (x2) ⁷_____ , ⁸_____
hot ⁹_____
small ¹⁰_____

**2** ★★☆ **Complete the sentences with extreme or ordinary adjectives.**

1 The play wasn't funny – it was absolutely h_____ .
2 Their new baby isn't s_____ – it's really tiny.
3 Our holiday wasn't just good – it was w_____ .
4 I wasn't s_____ – I was absolutely terrified.
5 Marcus isn't sad about his exam result – he's really m_____ .
6 It isn't c_____ outside – it's absolutely freezing.
7 The new airport isn't big – it's absolutely h_____ .
8 The rollercoaster ride wasn't just e_____ – it was thrilling.
9 The book wasn't just i_____ – it was fascinating.
10 Our trip wasn't just g_____ , it was amazing!

**3** ★★☆ **Circle the correct word, a or b. If both are possible, choose c (*both*).**

1 We spent our holiday in Mexico and it was _____ boiling.
   a very   b absolutely   c *both*
2 Have you seen their new house? It's _____ enormous!
   a very   b absolutely   c *both*
3 I enjoyed the film. I thought it was _____ funny.
   a very   b absolutely   c *both*
4 Put a jacket on. It's _____ cold outside.
   a very   b really   c *both*
5 I think the idea of time travel is _____ fascinating.
   a very   b absolutely   c *both*
6 She's an artist. Her paintings are _____ good.
   a very   b really   c *both*

## *make* and *do*

→ SB p.61

**4** ★☆☆ **Complete the sentences with *make* or *do*.**

1 It just doesn't _____ any sense to me.
2 There must be easier ways to _____ money.
3 Maybe it's time to _____ some housework.
4 Can you _____ your own way here? I'm a bit busy at the moment.
5 I don't usually _____ this kind of experiment, but I don't see what could go wrong.
6 Jack's been quite lonely since his best friend moved away. We should _____ time to see him this weekend.

**5** ★★☆ **Match the sentences in Exercise 4 with the pictures.**

# REFERENCE

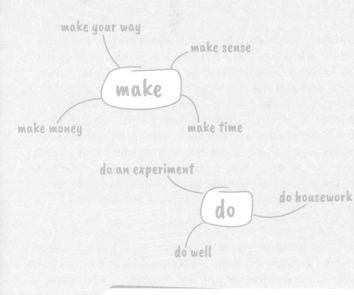

make
- make your way
- make sense
- make money
- make time

do
- do an experiment
- do housework
- do well

## MODIFIERS

absolutely     really     very

## EXTREME ADJECTIVES

| non-extreme | extreme |
|---|---|
| bad | awful, terrible |
| big | huge, enormous |
| cold | freezing |
| exciting | thrilling |
| funny | hilarious |
| good, great | fantastic, wonderful, brilliant, amazing |
| happy | delighted |
| hot | boiling |
| interesting | fascinating |
| sad | miserable |
| scared | terrified |
| small | tiny, minute |

# VOCABULARY EXTRA

**1  Look at the pictures and complete the phrases.**

fortune | mess | mistake

1  make a _____

2  make a _____

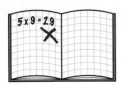

3  make a _____

badly | best | research

4  do _____

5  do _____

6  do your _____

**2  Complete the sentences with the phrases in Exercise 1. Use the correct form of make or do.**

1  Lexi's in the library. She _____
   for the Science project.

2  The Howard family worked hard at their business
   and they _____ .

3  I _____ such
   _____ in the kitchen when
   I tried that new recipe!

4  Brady _____ in the race.
   He came last.

5  The important thing is to
   _____ even if you don't always
   get good marks.

6  I'm sorry, I _____ . I thought
   you were someone else.

**3  Complete the sentences with your own ideas.**

1  If I made a fortune, I would _____ .

2  In my family, _____ makes the most
   mess because _____ .

3  I'd like to do research into _____ .

4  If I always did my best at school, _____ .

5  The worst mistake I ever made was when
   _____ .

6  When my favourite team plays badly,
   I _____ .

# HOW DOES SHE DO IT?

 **1** _____

In March 2019, at the age of 21, Margo Hayes became the first woman to complete three of the world's toughest climbs when she successfully reached the top of Papichulo in Spain. She had already climbed La Rambla, Spain and Biografie, France in 2017. She was only 19 when she became the first woman to climb La Ramba, which is considered one of the hardest rock faces in the world to climb. It seems this young woman from Boulder, which means 'big rock', Colorado was certain to become a record-breaking climber.

 **2** _____

She comes from a family of climbers, so that helps! Her grandfather was the expedition leader on a new route to the top of Mount Everest in 1983 and her father has climbed many of the rock walls of Yosemite Valley, California. But that's not enough. Talent and training play an essential part. Margo was a talented gymnast and at the age of six, she was aiming for an Olympic gold medal. Unfortunately, she was forced to give up gymnastics because of an injury, but by the age of ten, she had joined Team ABC, a well-known training project for young climbers in Texas.

 **3** _____

You won't be surprised to hear that Margo is extremely ambitious and very serious about her sport. She always has new goals she wants to achieve. She organises her training and climbs with the greatest precision. She believes detailed planning before a climb is essential for success. You can't risk making mistakes when you're high up on a rock face. Before she starts a climb, she chooses the route and plans every move she'll make on the rock face. She says it's an incredible feeling to finish a climb that you have been imagining in your head for so long. She enjoys her climbs and loves the feel of the rock as well as the unique views of fantastic scenery. Reaching the top is a thrilling experience.

 **4** _____

Margo's quite small – only 160 cm tall and around 45 kg in weight – but she's strong and can move her body quickly and easily into any position. She's sure that her gymnastics training has helped her climbing. She typically trains six days a week and spends 2–5 hours a day climbing both inside and outdoors. Running and working out in the gym are also included in her training programme. Her free time is spent mostly in the garden, where she keeps bees, but she also enjoys studying. She really likes Maths and Science.

What's her message for young climbers? 'Be curious and ask questions. Be kind and continually learn. Take risks and responsibility. Set goals and make a difference. Listen well and trust yourself.'

## 📖 READING

**1** **Read the article. Match the headings (a–d) with the paragraphs (1–4).**

- a Preparing the mind ...
- b How does she do it?
- c ... and the body
- d Making history

**2** **Read the article again. Correct the sentences.**

1 All Margo's record-breaking climbs were in Spain.

_____

2 She doesn't get ready for a climb in advance.

_____

3 She's the only one in her family who climbs.

_____

4 She has never tried any other sports.

_____

5 Margo spends all day, every day climbing.

_____

6 She discourages young people from doing her sport.

_____

**3** CRITICAL THINKING **Which statements would Margo probably agree with? Mark each statement yes (Y), no (N) or not sure (?). Give a reason.**

1 I often feel scared when I'm climbing. _____
Because _____

2 I decide how to climb a rock when I get there. _____
Because _____

3 Climbing is very hard work for the body and mind.
_____
Because _____

4 There's nothing better than the feeling when you reach the top. _____
Because _____

5 I advise young climbers to climb with other people.
_____
Because _____

PRONUNCIATION
The /ʒ/ phoneme  Go to page 119.

# DEVELOPING *Writing*

## Describing a process

**1** INPUT **Read the text and match the steps in the process (A–F) with the photos (1–6).**

# HOW YOUR PLASTIC WATER BOTTLE IS RECYCLED

If you can't avoid using a single-use plastic water bottle, the next best thing you can do is to recycle it. Find out about plastic recycling in your area. Do you have to put your bottle in a bin in the street or is plastic collected from outside your home? Find out which types of plastic can be recycled and follow the instructions carefully. Before sending your bottle for recycling, make sure it's clean.

**A** Next, the bottles are cleaned and the paper labels, glue and other non-plastic materials are removed.

**B** The plastic pellets are sold to companies and will be made into things like synthetic clothes, floor mats, furniture and even recycling bins!

**C** When the plastic bottles have been collected, they are transported to the recycling centre.

**D** After drying, the bottles are melted and finally, the plastic is formed into pellets.

**E** The plastic is now broken down into tiny pieces and washed again because it must be perfectly clean.

**F** The bottles are sorted by machine into different bins depending on the type of plastic they are made from. Most bottles are made from PET. So, your water bottle goes with all the other objects made of this type of plastic. Plastics that can't be dealt with at the centre are sent to other specialised recycling centres.

**2** ANALYSE **Match the words from the article (1–5) with the definitions (a–e).**

1 pellets ☐
2 melt ☐
3 sort ☐
4 process ☐
5 break down ☐

a heat something solid until it becomes liquid
b reduce to small pieces
c select and put with similar things
d small, hard pieces
e a series of actions

**3** PLAN **Choose one of the processes below, or use your own idea. Do some research to find out about the process.**

- how bread is made
- how glass is recycled
- how ice cream is made

**4** **Use the information you have found to make a plan.**

What you need to do first of all: _____
Steps in the process: _____
_____
_____
What happens to the end product: _____

## PRODUCE

**5** PRODUCE **Write your description (about 200 words). Use your plan from Exercise 4. Make sure you include all the points in the checklist.**

### ✓ CHECKLIST

Organise the process into short steps.
Describe each step clearly.
Explain the process in the correct order.
Use verbs in the passive to describe the process.
Link the steps with words like *firstly, next, after that, finally*.

## 🎧 LISTENING

**1** 🔊 6.03 **Put the instructions for the card trick in order. Then listen and check.**

How to amaze your friends with a card trick:

- [ ] a 'I will now find your card from these ones on the table.'
- [ ] b 'Put your card on top of the bottom part of the pack.'
- [ ] c 'Choose any card from the pack. Don't tell me what it is.'
- [ ] d 'Is this your card?'

**2** 🔊 6.03 **Listen again. Complete the sentences with the missing sequencing words.**

1 _____ , ask your friend to choose a card and look at it secretly.

2 _____ , cut the pack of cards into two.

3 _____ , ask your friend to put the card on the top of the bottom part of the pack.

4 _____ , put the pack back together and go through the cards.

**3** 🔊 6.04 **Listen to the dialogue and put the pictures in order.**

How to pack a backpack.

A

C

B

D

**4** 🔊 6.04 **Listen again and complete the instructions.**

1 _____ , _____ the trainers with small thing like socks, then place them at the bottom of the bag.

2 _____ , _____ the T-shirts and then roll up each one tightly.

3 _____ _____ , _____ the rolls and place them on top of the trainers.

4 _____ , _____ them to fill in the empty spaces.

## DIALOGUE

**5** **Put the dialogue in the correct order.**

- [ ] Emma Five minutes. I'll remember that next time.
- [ ] Emma For about eight minutes.
- [ ] Emma No, I didn't. I didn't know I had to.
- [ ] Emma No, I didn't. I was far too hungry.
- [1] Emma Oh, dear. I've really made a mess of this egg. What did I do wrong?
- [ ] Tim Finally, did you wait for a minute before you started to eat it?
- [ ] Tim That's the first thing you should always do. How long did you cook it for?
- [ ] Tim That's far too long. Five minutes is all you need.
- [ ] Tim Did you wash the uncooked egg?

**6** **Complete the dialogue.**

> after | finally | first | now | then

**Millie** Hi, Mum. Are you having trouble with something?

**Mum** Yes, I want to post this photo online but I don't know how to do it.

**Millie** OK, let me help you. ¹_____ click here where it says 'photo/video'.

**Mum** Ah, OK.

**Millie** ²_____ that, click on 'upload photo'. Great! ³_____ it's asking you which photo you want to upload.

**Mum** OK. I want this one here.

**Millie** OK, so just double-click on that. And ⁴_____ write something about the photo if you want.

**Mum** All right.

**Millie** And ⁵_____ click on 'post' and that's it! You've finished!

# TOWARDS B2 First for Schools

## READING AND USE OF ENGLISH
### Multiple choice

1   You are going to read an extract from *The Mind Map*. For questions 1–4, choose the answer
(A, B, C or D) which you think fits best according to the text. Look back at the exam guide
in Unit 5 on how to answer this question type.

### The Mind Map by David Morrison

Eva was thinking hard. She looked past Lucho. He turned and saw that she was looking at a little yellow bird which had landed on the grass behind him.

'I've seen this bird a lot recently,' he said. 'Maybe it's trying to help me.'

Eva corrected him, 'Maybe it's trying to help us, Lucho.'

Lucho smiled.

'Come on,' he said. 'Let's follow it.'

Lucho pulled Eva up by the hand and they followed the little bird over the grass, towards the door to the school building. When they reached the door, Mr Parra, the History teacher, was walking out of the building.

'How is your mind map going, you two?' Mr Parra asked.

Lucho was not sure what to say. They couldn't tell Mr Parra that the mind map seemed to be alive.

'It's going well, sir,' said Eva, 'but we've got a question to ask you. Do you know what "Ichua" means?'

Mr Parra smiled.

'Ichua is the name of the most important place in the world for the Kogi,' he explained. 'Their most important chiefs are buried there. The Kogi say it is a secret underground place full of gold, but historians don't believe that it's a real place. I see you have spent your time well in the library.'

It was Lucho's turn to ask a question. 'Mr Parra, do you know if there is a hotel in Santa Marta called the Hotel Continental?'

'Why?' Mr Parra was laughing. 'Are you planning a holiday?'

'No, sir,' answered Lucho, feeling a little stupid.

'Well, there was a hotel called the Hotel Continental in Santa Marta, near the port. But it closed a few years ago,' Mr Parra explained.

Eva watched the little yellow bird fly up to the roof of the library.

'Any more questions?' Mr Parra asked.

'Yes,' said Eva. 'Are birds important in Kogi stories?'

'Oh yes, Eva. There is a bird in every Kogi story. A bird brings a message to the jaguar or it helps the jaguar in its work. The jaguar, of course, is the most important animal for the Kogi and for many other tribes. The jaguar looks after the Kogi. Without the help of the jaguar, the Kogi believe, the sun would not rise, plants would not grow and rain would not fall.'

Mr Parra smiled.

'I must say I am very pleased that you have been working so well. Don't forget to put all the information on your mind map and bring it to class on Monday.'

Eva and Lucho watched Mr Parra as he walked away from the school building. Lucho's head was full of questions. Had he dreamed that the mind map had grown? Had he added new words in his sleep? But then, why had the message 'TAKE IT BACK' appeared on the computer screen and on Eva's mobile phone? What did the pendant want? Did he have to take it back to Ichua? But how could he? Mr Parra had said that Ichua probably wasn't a real place.

1   Eva corrects Lucho about the bird because …
    A   he doesn't know what kind of bird it is.
    B   she wants him to know that she's going to help him.
    C   he misunderstands how the bird is trying to help them.
    D   she thinks they should follow it.

2   Which of these statements is not true about Mr Parra?
    A   He is one of their teachers at the school.
    B   He gave Lucho and Eva the mind map homework.
    C   He is pleased the students are taking their homework seriously.
    D   He was walking in the same direction as Lucho and Eva.

3   What do we learn about the Kogi from their stories?
    A   They are the only tribe for whom the jaguar is important.
    B   They like birds, especially yellow ones.
    C   There are jaguars in all their traditional stories.
    D   Nature is a very important part of their culture.

4   What does the final paragraph suggest about Lucho?
    A   He thinks he might be doing things in his sleep.
    B   He wanted to ask Mr Parra more questions.
    C   He's sure that he's started to imagine things.
    D   He's really confused about the mind map mystery.

# CONSOLIDATION

## 🎧 LISTENING

1 🔊 6.05 **Listen and circle the correct option: A, B or C.**

1 How long did the story for homework have to be?
   A 50,000 words
   B 5,000 words
   C 500 words

2 What did the story have to be about?
   A ghosts
   B crime
   C romance

3 If the teacher likes his story, the boy might …
   A help the girl to write one.
   B send it to a website.
   C publish it in the school magazine.

2 🔊 6.05 **Listen again and answer the questions.**

1 Why does the boy enjoy homework that involves writing a story?

   _____

2 How does he usually get an idea for a story?

   _____

3 How long did he spend writing the story?

   _____

4 Where did he get the idea for the story from?

   _____

5 What does the girl want the boy to do?

   _____

## Ⓖ GRAMMAR

3 **Circle the correct options.**

1 There was an accident and a lot of people *hurt / were hurt*.

2 These books *are written / were written* a very long time ago.

3 The new school *will be opened / will open* by the mayor tomorrow.

4 I don't understand computers, so I always *repair my computer / have my computer repaired* when there's a problem.

5 In the last two years, they *have built / have been built* a lot of new buildings here.

6 I went to the hairdresser's and *cut my hair / had my hair cut*.

7 Thirty people *have taken / have been taken* to hospital.

8 Doctors *operate / are operated* on more than 30 people here every day.

4 **Complete the sentences with *who, whose, where, that* or *which*.**

1 That's the school _____ Dad taught.

2 Mr Newson, my Maths teacher, is someone _____ I've learned a lot from.

3 I've forgotten _____ book this is.

4 Newquay, _____ is a small town in the south of England, is where my sister lives.

5 Careful, it's the dog _____ tried to bite me.

6 Look, that's the guy _____ was on the news last night.

## 🔤 VOCABULARY

5 **Complete the dialogue.**

> characters | crime | ending
> hero | plot | setting | villain

**Alex**    I read a good book last week. It was called *Detective Grange Investigates*.

**Giorgia** What's it about?

**Alex**    Well, it's a ¹_____ novel. The ²_____ is London at the end of the 19th century. And of course the ³_____ of the story is Detective Grange.

**Giorgia** And what's the ⁴_____ ?

**Alex**    Well, it's about how Grange finds out who stole some money from a rich family's house. Grange meets all kinds of different people – there are some funny ⁵_____ and some horrible ones! The worst person is Dangerous Dan – he's the ⁶_____ of the story. At the end …

**Giorgia** No, no! Don't tell me the ⁷_____ ! I might read the book myself!

6 **Complete the words.**

1 I thought the play was a_____ fantastic.

2 Some of the things were so funny – in fact, they were h_____ .

3 One actor said something that didn't make s_____ to me, but it didn't matter.

4 One actress was very young, but she did very well – she was b_____ , in fact.

5 She took the part of the evil v_____ in the play.

6 We were all very happy that we saw the play – in fact, we were d_____ !

7 The theatre was very big – I've never seen such an e_____ theatre in my life!

8 It was a bit noisy, so sometimes I couldn't hear the d_____ between the actors very well.

## DIALOGUE

**7** 🔊 6.06 **Complete the conversation with the phrases in the list. There are two extra phrases. Then listen and check.**

> it isn't strange | let me finish | the strangest thing happened
> what are the chances | you'll never believe | what's strange
> that was the annoying thing | I don't understand

**Jay** ¹_____ to me last weekend. I had a dream on Sunday about being lost in a completely empty city.

**Sara** ²_____ about that? People have dreams all the time – including about being lost.

**Jay** I know. But the next day on TV there was a film where a woman was lost in an empty city, too – just like my dream. ³_____ of that happening?

**Sara** Well, not huge, I suppose. But it's only a coincidence, isn't it?

**Jay** Well, ⁴_____ . There's more! You see, in the film, when the woman was lost, she started to hear a loud noise, like a wild animal or something. And ⁵_____ what happened next! A tiger suddenly appeared in front of her! Now, in my dream, I started to hear a strange noise, too!

**Sara** And did a tiger appear in your dream?

**Jay** Well, ⁶_____ . You see, just when the noise started, I woke up! So I don't know if there was a tiger in my dream or not. But my cat was lying on my bed!

## 📖 READING

**8** **Read the book review. Choose the correct answer (A, B or C).**

1 What kind of stories was Paul Auster looking for?
   A real stories that weren't too long
   B the listeners' favourite stories
   C true stories about famous people

2 Why did he decide to put the stories in the book?
   A because he wanted to share them all with the public
   B to make some money
   C because he couldn't read them all out on the radio

3 What does the reviewer recommend?
   A to read the book from start to finish
   B to pick and choose stories from the book
   C to only read the sections you are most interested in

4 What is the reviewer's overall opinion of the book?
   A She liked it because the stories are so well written.
   B She liked it because some of the stories are very moving.
   C She liked another book of real-life stories more.

## Review:
### True Tales of American Life

In 1999, the writer Paul Auster was asked if he would contribute stories to America's National Public Radio. But Auster decided to ask listeners to send in their stories instead. He wanted true stories that sounded more like fiction. They could be about anything at all; they just had to be true and short. The chosen ones would be read out on the radio.

To Auster's surprise, more than 4,000 listeners sent in their stories. It would have been impossible to read them all on the radio, so Auster took almost 200 stories and put them together – and this is the book.

I liked some things about the collection, but others not so much. Because the stories were written by ordinary people, they aren't always well written (I hate to think what the ones that weren't included were like!). And I didn't think the categorisation into sections like Families, Objects, Strangers, or Animals worked. It means that if you read one story after the other, it can become a bit repetitive. What's more, some of the stories fall into more than one category.

As with any book of short stories, they don't have to be read in a particular order. You can just choose one here and there whenever you feel like it. You don't have to read the whole book straight through, and that's probably the best thing to do here, too.

What's great about these stories is their veracity – they're all true, no matter how unbelievable (and some of them really are incredible). One or two of the stories left me almost in tears, they were so moving.

So, overall, it's worth buying and reading. If you're into real-life stories like these, I'd also recommend a collection called *The Moth* – more on that next time.

## ✏️ WRITING

**9** **Write a review of a story that you like (from a film, TV programme, book, or even a true story about you or a friend). Write 150–200 words.**

# 7 BREAKING AWAY

## Ⓖ GRAMMAR

*make / let* and *be allowed to*  → SB p.68

**1** ⭐☆☆ **Complete the sentences with *make* or *let*.**

Here is what life is like at the summer camp. Some things are great – others, not so much!

1 They _____ us watch TV every evening until 10.30.

2 They _____ us clean our shoes every day.

3 They _____ us tidy the things in our room at the end of every day.

4 They _____ us check our phones twice a day.

5 They _____ us spend our free time in our rooms.

6 They _____ us take a cold shower every day.

7 They _____ us sleep late on Saturdays and Sundays.

8 They _____ us eat vegetables with every meal.

**2** ⭐⭐☆ **Rewrite the sentences using *make / doesn't make / lets / doesn't let*.**

0 **Mum**  You have to wash up after dinner.
*Mum makes me wash up after dinner.*

1 **Dad**  You can stay out later on Saturdays.
_____

2 **Mum**  You can't play loud music in the house.
_____

3 **Mum**  You don't have to tidy your room.
_____

4 **Mum**  You don't have to get up early on Sundays.
_____

5 **Dad**  You can't drive my car.
_____

6 **Dad**  You have to put the rubbish out.
_____

7 **Dad**  You can invite friends round at the weekend.
_____

**3** ⭐⭐⭐ **Look at the signs. Rewrite them using *You're (not) allowed to.***

0 *You're not allowed to cycle here.*

No cycling

1 _____
_____

NO FOOD AND DRINK IN THIS ROOM

2 _____
_____

SWITCH OFF YOUR MOBILE PHONE

3 _____
_____

Fill up your water bottle here. Free

4 _____
_____

NO NOISE AFTER 9 PM

5 _____
_____

PHONE CHARGING POINT

6 _____
_____

No entry to under-16s

7 _____
_____

LIBRARY: no more than 4 books at a time

**4** ⭐⭐⭐ **Complete the sentences so that they are true for you.**

1 I'm not allowed to _____

2 My friends never let me _____

3 At school, we're allowed to _____

4 Our teacher doesn't let us _____

5 I don't like it when someone makes me
_____

6 It isn't fair to make someone
_____

5 ★★★ **Make questions using the prompts and make / let / be allowed to.**

0 parents / you / help with the housework?

*Do your parents make you help with the*
*housework?*

1 teachers / you / do homework every night?

_____

2 you / send messages in class?

_____

3 school / you / go into any room you want?

_____

4 parents / you / sleep as long as you like?

_____

5 you / eat anything you want at home?

_____

6 parents / you / stay out after midnight?

_____

6 ★★★ **Write your answers to the questions in Exercise 5.**

0 _____
1 _____
2 _____
3 _____
4 _____
5 _____
6 _____

## be / get used to

→ SB p.69

7 ★☆☆ **Match the parts of the sentences.**

1 When we went to Boston, it took us time ☐
2 She was a bit nervous because ☐
3 It isn't always easy ☐
4 At first Mum didn't like working from home, ☐
5 My brother is learning Arabic and he has to ☐
6 When my sister joined the police, she ☐
7 He didn't like the cat at first because ☐
8 Can I have a knife and fork, please? ☐

a she wasn't used to travelling alone.
b get used to writing from right to left.
c had to get used to wearing a uniform.
d to get used to the American accent.
e he was used to having dogs at home.
f I'm not used to using chopsticks.
g but then she got used to it.
h to get used to life in a different country.

8 ★★☆ **Complete the sentences with *be used to* or *get used to* and the correct form of a verb from the list.**

eat | go | live | (not) hug | read

1 Before I went to China, I _____
with a knife and fork, but then
I _____ with chopsticks.

2 Back home, when I had a job,
I _____ to work by train,
so I had to _____ to work by
bus in China.

3 I also had to _____ people
very much – it wasn't easy because in my country,
we _____ our family and
friends a lot!

4 And of course in my language,
I _____ things in the Roman
alphabet, but when I started to learn Chinese, I had
to _____ Chinese characters.

5 So now I _____ in China,
but I won't live here forever – in two years, I'll go
back home, I think.

## GET IT RIGHT!

### be used to vs. get used to

**Learners have difficulty in telling the difference between *be used to something* and *get used to something*.**

**We use *be used to* to say that we are familiar with something now.**

✓ *My friends in Spain find it strange that we eat dinner at 6 pm, but it's normal for us. We're used to it.*

✗ *My friends in Spain find it strange that we eat dinner at 6 pm, but it's normal for us. We get used to it.*

**We use *get used to* to talk about the process of becoming familiar with something over time.**

✓ *When I first came to the UK, I found it strange to eat dinner at 6 pm, but after a while I got used to it.*

✗ *When I first came to the UK, I found it strange to eat dinner at 6 pm, but after a while I am used to it.*

(Circle) **the correct words.**

1 Swimming practice was hard at first, but I *am / got* used to it eventually.

2 It's easy to get up at 8 am, now that I'm / got used to it.

3 I finally *am / got* used to the rain in Manchester after a few months.

4 At first, he didn't like his new school, but after a few weeks he *is / got* used to it.

5 Ciara didn't understand her new Spanish teacher, but now she *is / got* used to her accent.

6 *Are / Did* you get used to the food there eventually?

 **VOCABULARY**
Phrasal verbs (1)

→ SB p.68

1 ⭐☆☆ **Match the verbs (1–8) with their definitions (a–h).**

| | |
|---|---|
| 1 turn down | a stop doing something (often a bad habit) |
| 2 take up | b discover |
| 3 show up | c start a journey |
| 4 give up | d refuse or say no to someone |
| 5 carry on | e begin (a hobby or new subject) |
| 6 find out | f arrive at a place after a long time (after some time or effort) |
| 7 end up | g continue |
| 8 set off | h arrive at a place (often late or unexpectedly) |

2 ⭐⭐☆ **Complete the sentences with the correct forms of the phrasal verbs in Exercise 1.**

1 They were so late! We agreed to meet at 7.30 but they didn't _____ until 8.15!

2 We started playing at three in the afternoon, and we _____ until it got dark.

3 Sam was so happy when he _____ that he'd won the competition.

4 After a while trying to find the house, we _____ getting there too late for the party!

5 I'm really sorry but I have to _____ your invitation. I'm busy on Saturday.

6 We _____ at eight in the morning and by midday, we were at the seaside!

7 The exam was too hard! After 20 minutes I _____ and left the room.

8 My dad was getting bored at home, so he _____ golf and now he's out all the time.

Personality

→ SB p.71

3 ⭐☆☆ **Complete the puzzle.**

1 It was very _____ of you to offer to help.

2 I didn't like him – he was very _____ .

3 I like her – she's a very _____ person.

4 It's 'me, me, me' all the time – she's so _____ .

5 I like her smile – it's so _____ and welcoming.

6 He always says things nicely – he's very _____ .

7 Please don't laugh at me – it's very _____ .

8 She won't come and talk to you – she's too _____ .

|   |   |   |   |   |   |   |   |   |
|---|---|---|---|---|---|---|---|---|
| 1 |   |   |   | G |   |   |   |   |
| 2 |   |   |   | E |   |   |   |   |
| 3 |   |   |   | N |   |   |   |   |
| 4 |   |   |   | E |   |   |   |   |
| 5 |   |   |   | R |   |   |   |   |
| 6 |   |   |   | O |   |   |   |   |
| 7 |   |   |   | U |   |   |   |   |
| 8 |   |   |   | S |   |   |   |   |

4 ⭐⭐☆ **Complete the sentences with personality adjectives. Start each adjective with the first letter of the person's name.**

1 Layla is _____

2 Chris is _____

3 Simon is _____

4 Gisella is _____

WordWise:
Phrases with *all*

→ SB p.69

5 ⭐⭐☆ **Complete the sentences with the correct phrase with *all* from the list.**

| all day | all I'm saying | all the same |
|---|---|---|
| for all I know | once and for all | after all |

1 Of course I'll help you. _____ , you're my friend!

2 I've been working on this problem _____ – I'm tired!

3 **A** Who's that guy over there?
   **B** I've got no idea. He could be anyone, _____ .

4 You've asked me that question five times! _____ , I don't know – OK?

5 Look, I know it's your favourite film. _____ is that I didn't like it.

6 Well, we can go to the sports centre or to the park. It's _____ to me.

 REFERENCE

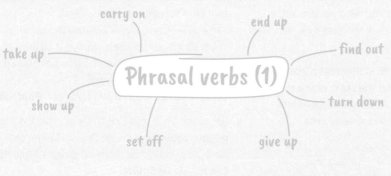

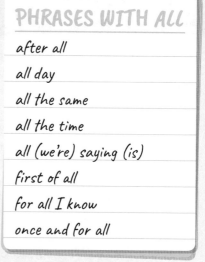

**PHRASES WITH ALL**

after all
all day
all the same
all the time
all (we're) saying (is)
first of all
for all I know
once and for all

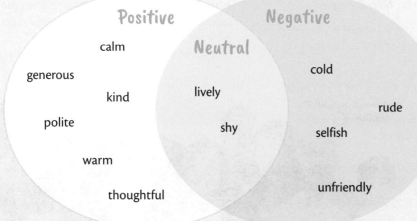

Positive
Negative
Neutral

calm
generous
kind
polite
warm
thoughtful

lively
shy

cold
rude
selfish
unfriendly

 **VOCABULARY** *EXTRA*

1 **Mark the phrasal verbs in bold positive (✓), negative (✗) or neutral (N). Sometimes there is more than one correct answer.**

1 I spent all my money on clothes. They were all so cool, I just **got carried away**. _____
2 Asia often **lets** us **down**. She agrees to help and then doesn't show up. _____
3 We **look up to** Miss Jenkins. Everyone respects her. _____
4 Jacob thinks he's really important and **looks down on** other people. _____
5 The cost of my gym pass has increased, but I don't want to give it up. I'll just have to **put up with it**! _____
6 I can **rely on** Johnny because I know I can trust him. _____

2 **Put the words in order to make sentences.**

1 us / Thomas / to / we / on / help / always / rely / can
_____
2 on / down / classmates / Maya / her / looks /
_____
3 someone / teenagers / up / they / look / need / to / can
_____
4 I / my / never / let / friends / down
_____
5 with / mistakes / teacher / the / up / won't / put / spelling
_____
6 game / Harry / away / with / got / carried / the
_____

3 **Complete the sentences so that they are true for you.**

1 You can rely on me to _____
2 I sometimes get carried away when _____
3 My parents won't put up with _____
4 The person I look up to most is _____ because _____

# DAN'S DAILY
## Discussions

Last week, I asked you, my readers, to think about people and <sup>a</sup>stereotypes. I knew I could rely on you to send in some interesting ideas! This is what you came up with. I call this collection: _____ .

1 At the end of the day, we're all human beings, and that's that. The best way to <sup>b</sup>challenge stereotypes is just by being who you are and accepting others as they are. If we learn to do that, then we'll all get on better with each other. **Lia Cox**

2 I think people are all the same, really. We're born in different places and we have different cultures. We don't all look the same or speak the same language. But people are all the same, although we differ in hundreds of ways. That's what makes life so interesting! Let's celebrate our <sup>c</sup>diversity! **George Henderson**

3 Wasn't it the American writer Ernest Hemingway who said that everyone's life ends sooner or later? It's just how we live and how we die that <sup>d</sup>distinguish us from each other. **Mike Gillespie**

4 I think it's beautiful that everyone is different. If we were all the same, life would be very boring. We should allow everyone to live their lives in their own way. **Jenny Price**

5 My grandma always said that people are people. She always treated everyone in the same way and that's something we should all try to do. Too often, we let a person's appearance <sup>e</sup>influence what we think of them. We shouldn't look down on anyone because, in the end, we are all human beings and we should treat everyone equally. **Sarah White**

6 I forget who said, 'when it's dark, we're all the same.' I think this quotation is trying to remind us that people are basically all the same. It doesn't matter if someone is tall or short, young or old. We shouldn't judge people on their clothes, colour of their skin, what they believe or their culture. The main point is, though, that we all need to learn to put up with people who are different from us. That's the real problem. **Agata Morris**

7 The American President John F. Kennedy said that we share lots of things. We all live on the same planet, and we all breathe the same air. We think about our children's future. And we'll all die one day. The world would be a better place if we remembered this <sup>f</sup>quotation. JFK said a lot of wise things and I look up to him for this. **Paul Gibson**

8 Someone once said that there are two kinds of people: those who divide the world into two kinds of people, and those who don't. How true this is! **Janie Smith**

9 A friend of mine who had white hair when she was only 20 said, 'You laugh at me because I'm different. I laugh at you because you're all the same!' **Mandy Atkins**

## READING

1 **Read the comments on the blog page. Choose the title you think best fits the page.**

   A We are all the same
   B The same but different
   C Everyone is different

2 **Match the highlighted words in the blog page (a–f) with the definitions (1–6).**

   1 one or a few sentences taken from a book or play, or that were said by someone else ☐
   2 differences ☐
   3 fixed and often wrong ideas of what a person is like ☐
   4 question if something is true ☐
   5 recognise differences between two things ☐
   6 change what people think ☐

3 **Each of the writers agrees with one of the opinions below. Write the numbers (1–9) in the correct column.**

| We need to learn to accept each other. | Diversity is great and should be celebrated. |
|---|---|
| _____ | _____ |
| _____ | _____ |
| _____ | _____ |
| _____ | _____ |
| _____ | _____ |

4 **CRITICAL THINKING** **Underline** the sentence or phrase that best summarises the writer's opinion in each comment.

   1 _we're all human beings and that's that_

# DEVELOPING *Writing*

## A blog about a different country

**1** INPUT **Read the blog and tick (✓) the photos of the things that Francesca mentions.**

 A
 B
 C
 D
 E

**BLOG**   ABOUT   NEWS   ADVICE   GALLERY   CONTACT   🔍

**Here I am in Tanzania! We arrived a few weeks ago and we'll be staying for two years, so I'm going to write about my experiences – here's my first post.**

Dar es Salaam! ¹_____ , I love the place. It's wonderfully warm, but it gets humid sometimes and then you feel uncomfortable, but I'm slowly getting used to that. At this time of year, it rains every day for about an hour, usually in the afternoon. Sometimes it rains really hard! But when it stops, you get the wonderful smell of grass after summer rain.

²_____ , some things are different. Dar es Salaam isn't the capital, but it's a big city with over four million people living here – very different from our little town back home. There's one thing I'll never get used to: the huge traffic jams. It takes ages to drive anywhere. There's a cool atmosphere in the city: it's got an amazing cultural mix and the people are warm, friendly and calm – nobody ever seems to be in a hurry!

³_____ there's the food – it's all new for me, but delicious. My favourite is *Ndizi Kaanga* – that's fried green bananas.

⁴_____ I like most: it's the way people always shake hands when they meet. You must shake everyone's hand – even if there are 20 people – and you should start with the oldest person. It shows respect, which I think is wonderful.

⁵_____ , more in a week or two.

Bye for now,

Francesca

**2** ANALYSE **Read the blog again and answer the questions.**

1 How long is Francesca going to live in Dar es Salaam?
_____

2 What things does Francesca find very different in Tanzania?
_____
_____

3 Which thing(s) does she dislike? How do you know?
_____
_____

4 What is her favourite thing about Tanzania?
_____

**3** **Complete the blog with the phrases in the list.**

anyway | here's what | of course | so far | then

**4** PLAN **Imagine you have gone to live in another country. How is it different to your home country? Use the ideas in the blog to help you. Make a plan.**

things you're already used to: _____
things you don't like: _____
things you like: _____
the thing you like best: _____

**5** PRODUCE **Write a blog post (about 250 words) about your new country. Use your plan from Exercise 4. Make sure you include all the points in the checklist.**

 CHECKLIST

Explain which country you are in.
Say when you arrived and how long you are staying.
Give your general impression.
Say what you like best.

## LISTENING

**1** 🔊 **7.01** **Listen to three conversations.** Circle **the correct options.**

1 Sean *accepts* / *refuses* the invitation.

2 Eva *accepts* / *refuses* the invitation.

3 Bartie *accepts* / *refuses* the invitation.

**2** 🔊 **7.01** **Listen again and mark the sentences T (true) or F (false). Then correct the false sentences.**

1

a Sean is always busy at the weekend. ☐

b He isn't keen on films. ☐

c He accepts the invitation immediately. ☐

2

a Lucas invites Eva to a sports match. ☐

b Eva agrees to ask some of her friends to come, too. ☐

c Lucas gives Eva some advice about what to bring. ☐

3

a Bartie declines the invitation because he'll be away. ☐

b Helena suggests something else they can do. ☐

c Helena decides to change her plans for this evening. ☐

**3** 🔊 **7.01** **Listen again. Complete these parts of the dialogues.**

1

**Nadia** Well, listen, some of us are going to the cinema on Saturday. Why ¹_____ with us?

**Sean** No, wait, just a minute. I've changed my mind. ²_____ come. What time on Saturday?

**Nadia** I'm not sure yet, but it'll be in the evening. ³_____ me a call later when I've spoken to the others?

2

**Lucas** OK then. ⁴_____ along?

**Eva** ⁵_____ – I'd love to. I love walking. Thanks, Lucas.

**Lucas** No problem. ⁶_____ some friends along with you?

**Eva** OK, I'll call some people.

3

**Helena** We're thinking of going to the town festival tonight. There's a barbecue and live music in the park. Why ⁷_____ ?

**Bartie** I'd love to, but you'll have to ⁸_____ this time.

> **PRONUNCIATION**
> Intonation – inviting, accepting and refusing invitations **Go to page 120.** 🎧

## DIALOGUE

**4** **Put the dialogues in order.**

1

☐ **A** Well, how about coming with me to that new youth club in town?

☐ **A** Are you busy on Friday?

☐ **A** OK, let's meet there at seven.

☐ **B** Fine. I'll see you there.

☐ **B** That'd be great. I'd love to!

☐ **B** No, I'm not. Why?

2

☐ **C** Why don't you join us and bring someone along?

☐ **C** Do you fancy going to a party tonight?

☐ **C** A friend of mine, Jake. It's his birthday.

☐ **D** No, that's OK. I'd rather just go with you.

☐ **D** Whose party is it?

☐ **D** Yes, of course, thank you! I like parties.

## PHRASES FOR FLUENCY → SB p.72

**5** **Put the words in order to make phrases.**

0 point / good ___*good point*___

1 it / mention / don't _____

2 it / in / pack _____

3 it / one / in / got _____

4 me / don't / wrong / get _____

5 this / with / I'm / one / you / on _____

**6** **Complete the dialogues with phrases in Exercise 5.**

1 **A** It's great that you're helping me. Thanks a lot.

**B** Oh, _____ . It's a pleasure.

2 **A** Come on, let's go out for a walk.

**B** But the match is on TV in 15 minutes.

**A** Hmmm, _____ . Maybe we'll leave the walk until later.

3 **A** No, sorry – this music's really awful!

**B** _____ ,Tess. Let's listen to something else.

4 **A** So you didn't like the present I gave you?

**B** Oh, no. _____ , I liked it. It's just that red isn't my favourite colour.

5 **A** Mum, Angie won't give me my football back. Please tell her to.

**B** Oh, Rob, _____ , please! I've got a really bad headache.

6 **A** So, why can't you come out tonight? Homework?

**B** _____ . French, English and History!

# TOWARDS B2 First for Schools

## EXAM GUIDE

This tests your vocabulary, grammar and spelling. You have to complete a text with eight gaps. The base word is given at the end of the line and you have to transform it so that it fits into the sentence.

- First, read the text through for general meaning.
- Remember that the word you have to use is at the end of the line with the gap.
- You have to transform the base word into an adjective, noun or adverb of the same word family. For example, you may have to add a negative prefix and/or transform the word type using a suffix.
- Re-read the sentence containing the new word to make sure it makes sense.
- Check if nouns need to be singular or plural.
- Spelling is important. It must be correct.

1   For questions 1–8, read the text below. Use the word given in capitals at the end of some of the lines to form a word that fits in the gap in the same line. There is an example at the beginning (0).

**A Trip of a Lifetime!**

I'm not usually a very ⁰ _adventurous_ kind of person. I don't like having too much                    ADVENTURE
¹_____ in my life, but the trip that I took on the river at the Iguaçu Falls               EXCITE
between Brazil and Argentina was just fantastic and ² _____ unforgettable!          TOTAL
When you get close to the waterfalls, you get very wet from the spray. ³ _____ ,      FORTUNE
the day we went, it was cloudy, but we took some great photographs anyway.
The ⁴ _____ was spectacular.                                                        SCENE
Then we decided to go on a river trip to the falls. We got into an inflatable boat and sailed
up the river to the base of the waterfalls. The noise of the water was ⁵ _____          BELIEVE
loud! We had to be very ⁶ _____ and hold on tight because the water was rough.        CARE
A couple of times we were worried for our ⁷ _____ !                                  SAFE
When we returned to dry land, we all agreed it had been a memorable – but at times
⁸ _____ – trip!                                                                      SCARE

2   For questions 1–8, read the text below. Use the word given in capitals at the end of some of the lines to form a word that fits in the gap in the same line. There is an example at the beginning (0).

**Sea View Bed and Breakfast – a review**

We stayed here last month for three nights and had an ⁰ _enjoyable_ stay overall.            ENJOY
We really liked the location – it's in the town centre, so restaurants and shops are nearby.
There are very ¹ _____ views over the beach. Breakfast was good and healthy           ATTRACT
as it included a ² _____ of fresh fruit. Also, the staff could not have been more     SELECT
attentive and ³ _____ .                                                              FRIEND
The bedroom was large and ⁴ _____ , and so was the bathroom. So, what was            SPACE
the problem?
We had three almost ⁵ _____ nights. The bed was the hardest and most                 SLEEP
⁶ _____ bed I have ever tried to sleep in! The noise from the street outside          COMFORT
the window meant it was absolutely ⁷ _____ to get a good night's rest.                POSSIBLE
So, it's ⁸ _____ that we would go back. It's a shame because Sea View has            DOUBT
so many good things going for it.

# 8 CRIME AND PUNISHMENT

 Grammar rap! ▶21

## Ⓖ GRAMMAR
### Reported speech (review) → SB p.76

1 ★★☆ **Report what the burglar said to a police officer. Complete the sentences using reported speech.**

0 'I burgled a flat yesterday.'
He said ___he had burgled a flat the day___ before.

1 'I stole a laptop and some jewellery.'
He said _____
a laptop and some jewellery.

2 'I feel really terrible about stealing someone's things.'
He said _____
really terrible about stealing someone's things.

3 'I am going to say sorry to them.'
He said _____
sorry to them.

4 'I will never commit a crime again.'
He said _____
a crime again.

2 ★★☆ **Rewrite these sentences using reported speech.**

1 'I'm really upset,' said Mr Jones after the break-in.
_____

2 'The burglar broke into the house through the bathroom window,' a neighbour told the police.
_____

3 'This is the first time I've been caught shoplifting,' the boy told the store manager.
_____

4 'We were waiting on the underground platform when it happened,' said the students.
_____

5 'Pickpockets in London can make £4,000 a week by stealing wallets, smartphones and laptops,' a police officer told us.
_____

6 'I will think about putting security cameras in the shop,' the shopkeeper said after the robbery.
_____

7 'My son is going to report the mugging to the police,' said Mrs Roberts.
_____

3 ★★☆ **Rewrite what the people said in direct speech.**

0 The residents asked the police if they had arrested the mugger yet.
_Have you arrested the mugger yet?_

1 The security guard told the police that he had seen the shoplifter run across the car park.
_____
_____

2 The thief told the police officer that he had never been arrested before.
_____
_____

3 The police officer asked a neighbour if anybody was living in the house next door.
_____
_____

4 The lawyer told the gang that they would probably be sentenced to three years in prison.
_____
_____

5 The woman said that she was going to report the scam to the police.
_____
_____

### Reported questions, requests and imperatives → SB p.77

4 ★☆☆ **Circle the correct options.**

1 'Sit down.'
The police officer told me *sit down / to sit down*.

2 'Write your statement on the form.'
She told me *write / to write* my statement on the form.

3 'Don't worry.'
She told me *not to worry / don't worry*.

4 'Did you see the thief?'
She asked me if I *had seen / saw* the thief.

5 'Do you live in this block of flats?'
She asked me whether I *lived / had lived* in this block of flats.

6 'Are you going to interview anyone else?'
I asked her if she *had interviewed / was going to interview* anyone else.

**5**  ⭐⭐☆  **Complete the sentences.**

1  'Write down your name and address.'

He asked me _____

_____

2  'Stand up.'

She told us _____

_____

3  'Do you know the victim?'

He asked us _____

_____

4  'Describe the mugger.'

He asked me _____

_____

5  'Fill in the form.'

She told him _____

_____

6  'Have you been burgled before?'

He asked her _____

_____

**6**  ⭐⭐☆  **Match the sentences (1–8) with the sentence beginnings (a–h). Then complete the sentences.**

1  'No, I won't tell you where we've hidden the phones,' said the boy.  ☐

2  'Where did you hide the phones?' asked the police officer.  ☐

3  'No, I was in the car when they hid the phones,' said the boy.  ☐

4  'Come to the police station and make a statement,' said the police officer.  ☐

5  'You must tell me who the other two boys are,' said the police officer.  ☐

6  'All right. I'll come to the police station with you,' said the boy.  ☐

7  'Can I phone my mum?' asked the boy.  ☐

8  'Do you have a phone?' asked the police officer.  ☐

a  The boy asked if

_____

b  The police officer told the boy

_____

c  The police officer demanded to know

_____

d  The boy refused to tell the police

_____

e  The police officer asked the boy where

_____

f  The police officer asked the boy if

_____

g  The boy explained that

_____

h  The boy agreed

_____

**7**  ⭐⭐⭐  **Read the script for a play. Then report the dialogue.**

*Mark is waiting for the bus when a guy walks up to him.*

**Mugger**  Do you want to survive tonight?

**Mark**  I don't understand what you mean.

**Mugger**  The night can have a good ending or a bad ending. It's up to you.

**Mark**  Please tell me what you mean by that. Are you a mugger? I've only got £20.

**Mugger**  That's fine.

*[Mark gives him the money. The mugger moves closer. Mark is scared.]*

**Mark**  Are you going to hurt me?

**Mugger**  Thanks, mate.

*[hugs the boy and walks off]*

*Mark was surprised – he couldn't believe that the mugger had hugged him!*

He asked me [1] _____

I told him I [2] _____

He said that the night [3] _____

I asked him [4] _____

I wanted to know [5] _____

I told him that [6] _____

He said that [7] _____

I asked him [8] _____

## GET IT RIGHT!

### Reported questions

**In reported questions, we don't use question word order, but statement word order.**

✓  *I'll ask where I can find the station.*

✗  *I'll ask where can I find the station.*

**We don't need the auxiliary *do*.**

✓  *They asked when it started.*

✗  *They asked when did it start.*

**If it is a yes / no question, we need to include *if*.**

✓  *I'll ask if he has arrived yet.*

✗  *I'll ask he has arrived yet.*

**Correct the sentences.**

1  He asked how much did I pay for the phone.

_____

2  Everyone asked when did the article have to be finished.

_____

3  I asked my mum I could go out.

_____

4  I asked my parents which school will I go to when we move house.

_____

 **VOCABULARY**
**Crime**

→ SB p.76

1 ⭐☆☆ **Complete the sentences with the correct word or phrase from the list.**

> arrested | breaking in | committing a crime
> fine | got caught | got into trouble
> murder | murderers | prison | prisoner

1 The punishment for some minor crimes is paying a ¹_____ instead of going to ²_____ .

2 An escaped ³_____ was ⁴_____ again this morning as he was ⁵_____ .
He ⁶_____ while he was stealing a car.

3 A man nearly ⁷_____ with the police when they saw him climbing into a house through the window. They thought he was ⁸_____ , but he'd just forgotten his key.

4 ⁹_____ is a very serious crime and ¹⁰_____ are often sent to prison for life.

2 ⭐⭐☆ **Put the pictures about the story of Bob the burglar in order. Then write the story with some of the words and phrases in Exercise 1.**

_____
_____
_____
_____

_____
_____
_____
_____

_____
_____
_____
_____

_____
_____
_____
_____

3 ⭐⭐☆ **Read the clues and complete the puzzle.**

1 a building where criminals are kept as a punishment
2 a person who kills another person
3 to enter a building illegally with the intention of stealing
4 money that has to be paid for breaking a rule or law
5 a person who has been put in prison
6 The mugger got _____ by the police and taken away.
7 If you _____ a crime, you will be punished.
8 the crime of killing another person
9 The robbers broke _____ the bank through a tunnel.
10 The police _____ a person when they know or think they have broken the law.

|   |   | P |   |   |   |   |
|---|---|---|---|---|---|---|
|   | 2 | U |   |   |   |   |
| 3 |   | N |   |   |   |   |
|   | 4 | I |   |   |   |   |
| 5 |   | S |   |   |   |   |
| 6 |   | H |   |   |   |   |
| 7 |   | M |   |   |   |   |
| 8 |   | E |   |   |   |   |
| 9 |   | N |   |   |   |   |
| 10 |   | T |   |   |   |   |

**Reporting verbs**

→ SB p.79

4 ⭐⭐☆ **Circle the correct words.**

1 'I won't go to the police station.'
The boy *refused* / *agreed* to go to the police station.

2 'I was in the garden when it happened.'
The woman *refused* / *explained* that she had been in the garden when it happened.

3 'Yes, you're right. It's my fault.'
The girl *agreed* / *recommended* that it was her fault.

4 'I need you to tell me what happened.'
The man *told* / *demanded* to know what had happened.

5 'I was with my friends at a club at 9 pm last night.'
The man *claimed* / *agreed* that he had been with his friends at a club at 9 pm that night.

6 'Empty your pockets for me, please.'
The police officer *explained* / *told* him to empty his pockets.

7 'We're going to the park. Would you like to come with us?'
They *persuaded* / *invited* me to go to the park with them.

8 'If you like pizza, then Pizza Shed on the High Street is the place to go.'
She *recommended* / *invited* having pizza at Pizza Shed.

9 'I know it's hard, but I think you should try to learn Japanese.'
He *invited* / *encouraged* me to learn Japanese.

10 'OK, OK, I'll go to the concert with you.'
I *persuaded* / *agreed* her to go to the concert with me.

# REFERENCE

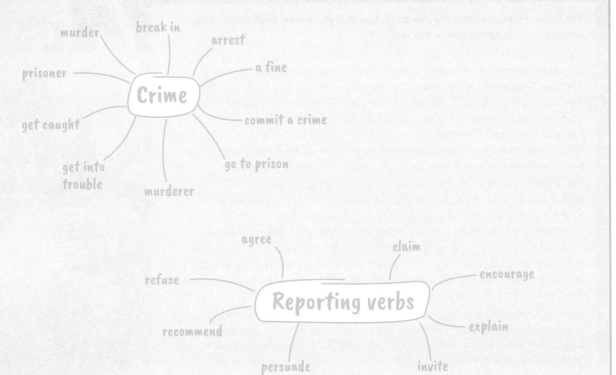

# VOCABULARY *EXTRA*

**1** Complete the table with the verbs in the list.

arrest | mug | murder | pickpocket
punish | shoplift | steal | suspect

| Crime verbs | Other verbs |
|---|---|
| murder | arrest |
| | |
| | |
| | |

**2** Match the verbs (1–6) with the phrases (a–f).

1 to mug ☐
2 to pickpocket ☐
3 to punish ☐
4 to shoplift ☐
5 to steal ☐
6 to suspect ☐

a a video game from a store
b a wallet on the underground
c a car from outside a house
d a criminal for a crime
e a person in the street
f someone of a crime

**3** Choose one of the groups of words and write a short story using them.

**A**

arrest | pickpocket | steal

**B**

get into trouble | shoplift | suspect

_____
_____
_____
_____
_____
_____
_____
_____
_____
_____
_____
_____
_____
_____

# A life of crime ...
# IN THE ANIMAL KINGDOM

**We love animals, especially our pets, but did you know that these cute creatures sometimes break the law?**

Most cats catch birds and mice, then bring them home for their owners, but not Oscar the ginger cat. He steals from neighbours' gardens. Every day he arrives home with socks and underwear from washing lines, gardening gloves, toys and other small items. Oscar's owners don't know what to do. How do you stop a cat's criminal activities? They can't return the stolen goods because there are too many of them, and they don't know who they belong to. Instead, they've asked local residents to report missing items to them. They then invite the victims of Oscar's crimes to identify their belongings from among his collection.

Oscar's not the only cat with criminal habits. There's Birgit the cat in New Zealand, who specialises in stealing men's socks, and a cat called Sir-Whines-A-Lot in the US who steals money. He's an office cat and when customers are paying, he waits for an opportunity to take some banknotes. He was found out when an employee discovered a small pile of cash on the floor one morning. When the office explained what was happening on social media and that they'd given Sir-Whines-A-Lot's illegal earnings to charity, they received more contributions from their customers!

Anyone who's tried eating sandwiches on the beach will know that seagulls don't just eat fish. Seagulls are bigger than you might imagine and can become aggressive when they're trying to get your tasty snack. There's a seagull in Scotland that doesn't just steal food but shoplifts, too! This criminal bird regularly hangs out outside a bakery. He waits until there aren't any customers in the shop, then walks in, helps himself to a bag of crisps and carries it outside to eat. The owners are so used to it that they don't say anything anymore and the shoplifting seagull has become a local celebrity.

People say that the octopus is an intelligent animal, but Otto, who lives in an aquarium in Germany, has a criminal mind. He uses his intelligence to cause chaos. He regularly commits small crimes such as throwing rocks at the glass wall of his tank, but his most serious crime so far was to cause an electricity blackout in the aquarium on three nights in a row. Despite their investigations, the staff couldn't find the cause of the blackout. They agreed that the only solution was to spend the night in the aquarium and watch. That's how Otto got caught. When he climbed to the top of his tank and shot water at the light above it, the electricity was automatically switched off for safety.

Then there's the crow in Canada who disrupted a crime-scene investigation by flying away with a knife. The police reported that an officer had chased the bird until it dropped the knife!

And finally, there's Jack the husky in the US who has been banned from entering the state of Maryland, but nobody knows why!

 **READING**

1 **Read the article and tick (✓) the crimes mentioned.**

> burglary ☐ | murder ☐ | pickpocketing ☐
> shoplifting ☐ | theft ☐ | vandalism ☐

2 **Complete the sentences with the names of one or more of the animals in the article.**

1 _____ interrupted police work.

2 _____ has/have committed an unknown crime.

3 _____ is/are guilty of theft.

4 _____ has/have broken the law in several different ways.

5 _____ got caught while breaking the law.

6 _____'s crime had a positive result in the end.

3 CRITICAL THINKING **Read the article again and <u>underline</u> the sentences which contain extra information that is not absolutely necessary to understand the text.**

4 **Choose one of the animals in the article and write a short story written from their perspective.**

# DEVELOPING Writing

## An essay

**1** INPUT **Read the essay quickly. What is it about? Circle the best answer.**

A How crime makes people rich

B The reasons people become criminals

C The best way to prevent crime

# POVERTY IS THE CAUSE OF CRIME

**1** Crime is a serious problem in every country around the world. Some people think that one of the main causes of crime is poverty. Other people have claimed that poverty does not have a direct link to crime.

**2** ᵃ_____ , there are many reasons why people commit crimes, and poverty is one of them. For example, a teenager who has no money, but wants the same trainers as his or her classmates, goes out and shoplifts them.

**3** ᵇ_____ , it isn't just poor people who commit crimes. Wealthy people with good jobs, nice homes and loving families also break the law. However, they generally commit different types of crimes for a variety of reasons. ᶜ_____ , they may be risk-takers and enjoy the thrill. ᵈ_____ , children from a poor family with a very caring mother and father are unlikely to commit a crime. They have love and security, and they're happy.

**4** ᵉ_____ , the main reason for teenagers and young adults committing crimes is a lack of support from their families and people around them. They often feel unloved and they have few good role models.

**5** ᶠ_____ , poverty is undoubtedly a cause of crime, but it is not the only one. Governments need to improve living standards for all their citizens, and we must all try to give more support to children and teenagers in need.

**2** **Complete the essay with the phrases in the list.**

> firstly | for example | however | in my opinion
> on the other hand | to conclude

**3** ANALYSE **Read the essay again and match the headings with paragraphs 1–5.**

Argument for ☐        Argument against ☐

The conclusion ☐        Introduction presenting the issue ☐

The writer's opinion ☐

**4** PLAN **Think about the advantages and disadvantages of stricter punishments for criminals. Add two advantages and two disadvantages to each column.**

| Advantages | Disadvantages |
|---|---|
| It will discourage criminals from committing other crimes. | Sending someone to prison, where they mix with other criminals, will do more harm than good. |
| _____ | _____ |
| _____ | _____ |
| _____ | _____ |

**5** **Write a plan for the other paragraphs of the essay.**

• Introduction

• Your opinion

• Conclusion

**6** PRODUCE **Write an essay with the title 'Stricter punishments will reduce crime' (250 words). Use your plan from Exercises 4 and 5. Make sure you follow all the points in the checklist.**

✔ CHECKLIST

Use formal language.

Use the linking phrases in Exercise 2 to connect sentences and paragraphs.

Try to use vocabulary from the unit.

# 🎧 LISTENING

1 🔊 8.01 **Listen to the dialogue. Mark the sentences T (true) or F (false).**

1 A note came in the mail the other day for Jane. ☐
2 The note told Jane to collect a parcel from the post office. ☐
3 They wanted Jane to pay an extra £50. ☐
4 Jane never received the parcel. ☐
5 Jane's friend doesn't think it was a large amount of money. ☐
6 The police told her that hundreds of people had been tricked by the scam. ☐

2 🔊 8.01 **Listen again. Complete these parts of the dialogue.**

1
A You'll never guess what I've done.
B Uh oh, Jane, _____ !
A I've been really stupid.

2
A Yes, I paid it online. There was a website address and I paid immediately.
B Really? Were _____ a parcel?

3
B _____ ? Was the parcel delivered?
A No, it was a scam.
B _____ !
A There was _____ in the local newspaper the other day.

4
B Have you reported it to the police?
A Yes, I have. They told me that hundreds of people have been tricked.
B _____ !

3 🔊 8.02 **Listen to the dialogue between Kate and a police officer. Then answer the questions.**

1 Who stole Kate's bag?
_____

2 What did Kate say the girl looked like?
_____

3 Where was Kate's bag when it was stolen?
_____

4 What did the police officer advise Kate not to do?
_____

5 Why did the police officer tell Kate she should be careful with her bag?
_____

6 What did Kate say was in her bag?
_____

## DIALOGUE

4 **Complete the dialogues with the phrases in the list.**

> Tell me | No way | You'll never guess what
> Really | There was a story
> You won't believe what happened to
> That's awful | I heard a really sad story | What

1
A _____ happened to me!
B _____ ?
A I've won a short story writing competition.
B That's amazing. Well done.

2
C _____ yesterday.
D _____ .
C Mrs Price's cat disappeared last week and now Mrs Price is really lonely.
D _____ !

3
E _____ me last night.
F What?
E I fell asleep on the train and I didn't wake up until it got to London.
F _____ ! That's a long way from Oxford.

4
G _____ in the paper the other day about our Art teacher.
H _____ ?
G Yes, apparently, his grandfather was a famous artist. There's an exhibition of his paintings at the city centre art gallery next week.

5 **Write a short account of a time when you or someone you know had something stolen or was pickpocketed. Where were you/they? Who took it? What did they take?**

**PRONUNCIATION**
Intonation – expressing surprise
Go to page 120. 🎧

## WRITING
### An informal email or letter

## EXAM GUIDE

**Among the four questions to choose from, there is often an informal email or a letter. Your answer should be 140–190 words long.**

- Always write a brief plan before you start writing.
- Remember to start and close your email/letter correctly.
- Include <u>all</u> the information requested in the question.
- Choose an appropriate writing style for the person you are writing to.
- Keep within the word limit and remember you have about 40 minutes for each part of the Writing test.

1  **Read the exam task. <u>Underline</u> the important information.**

> **You have received an email from your English-speaking friend.**
>
> I've just heard that your bike's been stolen and I'm a bit concerned for you. When and where did it happen? How did you feel? How did you manage to get home? Did you report it to the police? Please let me know all the details.
> See you soon,
> Peter
>
> **Write your email in 140–190 words.**

2  **Read Anya's answer to the task. Which part of the question has she forgotten to answer?**

> ☂ **Anya**
>
> Great to hear from you, and thanks for your concern. Of course, I was very puzzled when I got to the bike rack and couldn't find my bike. Then I felt angry with the thief. How was I going to get home? I didn't have any money on me and it would take me ages to walk. Luckily, I always have my phone with me, so I rang my mum and explained to her what had happened. She told me to wait there and she'd come and pick me up. She said we could go together and report it to the headteacher.
>
> It's annoying because three other people have had their bikes stolen, too, and that's just in the last week! I really hope the school will do something about it.
>
> Oh – I'm sorry I have to go now. The police are here. The headteacher called them. I'll send you a message later to let you know what they say.
>
> Bye,
> Anya

3  **Look at the questions Anya asked herself before writing. Read the email again to find the answers.**

1  How did I feel when I first realised the bike was missing?

_____

2  Then, when I realised it had been stolen, how did I feel?

_____

3  How else could I get home?

_____

4  Who could come to help me?

_____

5  Who should I report the theft to?

_____

4  **Read the task and write your answer in 140–190 words.**

> **You have received an email from your English-speaking friend.**
>
> I'm so sorry to hear that you've been mugged. That's really awful! When and where did it happen? Were you hurt in the attack? How do you feel now? What did the mugger take? Did you report it to the police?
> Best,
> Theo
>
> **Write your email in 140–190 words.**

5  **Ask a friend to read your story and complete the sentences about it.**

I thought _____ was good.

I *thought / didn't think* the email explained everything.

You could improve it by _____

_____

_____

The language used was _____

_____

# CONSOLIDATION

##  LISTENING

**1** 🔊 8.05 **Listen and circle the correct option (A, B or C).**

1 How many times has the boy's bike been stolen?
  A twice in two years
  B three times in two years
  C twice in three years

2 Where was the bike stolen from?
  A inside a public garden
  B outside a car park
  C near some shops

3 Why is the boy going to the police station now?
  A to give a description of his bike
  B to help the police find it
  C to identify a bike they've found

**2** 🔊 8.05 **Listen again. Complete each sentence with between two and four words.**

1 The boy got the money to buy his bike by cutting _____ cars.

2 The boy had _____ on it but the thieves cut it off.

3 His bike was stolen in _____ .

4 The boy doesn't think the police are _____ his bike.

5 The police have got _____ station that fits the description.

## 🅖 GRAMMAR

**3** **Circle the correct options.**

1 George told me *to leave / leave* right away.

2 We aren't *allow / allowed* to go into the lab without permission.

3 I don't think I'll ever get used to *drive / driving* on the left.

4 Does your school *make / let* you wear anything you want?

5 Lots of people don't like the weather here, but they soon *are / get* used to it.

6 I never want to get up at six o'clock, but my parents *let / make* me.

7 The new student asked me where *I was from / was I from.*

8 The teacher encouraged us *to take / taking* the exam.

9 I invited Lily *to come / come* with us.

10 Tina asked us what *did we have / we had* to do.

**4** **Complete the sentences using the correct form of the word in brackets.**

0 My dad says I have to get up at 7.00. (make)
  *My dad makes me get up at 7.00.*

1 Our teacher says it's OK to use a dictionary. (let)
  Our teacher _____ .

2 We can't go into that room. (allowed)
  We _____ .

3 The headteacher told us to clean the playground. (make)
  The headteacher _____ .

4 Last week our mum said we couldn't watch TV. (let)
  Our mum _____ .

## 🄰z VOCABULARY

**5** **Complete the phrasal verbs.**

1 Yesterday I just hung _____ with my friends.

2 Could you look _____ my cat while I'm away at the weekend?

3 What time does the plane take _____ ?

4 Grandad decided to take _____ playing the piano when he was 60.

5 My sister and I have always got _____ well together.

6 We didn't want to stop, so we just carried _____ walking.

7 I waited for hours but Maxine didn't show _____ .

8 My mum gave _____ eating meat years ago.

**6** **Complete each sentence with one word.**

1 If you break that window, you'll get into _____ with the neighbours.

2 I don't mind what we listen to. It's all the _____ to me.

3 Anna had to pay a _____ because she parked in the wrong place.

4 I don't know anyone who has ever _____ a crime.

5 She stole some money and went to _____ for three months.

6 There was a _____-in at the supermarket. The thieves stole a lot of food and money.

7 The thief was _____ while he was cutting through the bike lock.

8 Hey, stop asking me that question! _____ and for all, I don't know!

9 Harry always says 'please' and 'thank you'. He's so _____ .

10 Camilla only thinks about herself. She's really _____ .

## DIALOGUE

7  🔊 8.06  **Complete the conversation with the phrases in the list. Then listen and check.**

> be honest │ don't mention it │ I know how you feel
> get me wrong │ I'm with you │ in fact
> it in one │ point

**Tessa**  Here's your satnav back. Thanks a lot for lending it to me.

**Jack**  ¹_____ . I hope it was useful.

**Tessa**  Yes, it was, thanks. But listen, Jack – don't ²_____ , but maybe you should get a new one.

**Jack**  Why? Is it out of date?

**Tessa**  Yes! Got ³_____ . I mean, it was useful, like I said. But three times it tried to make us drive the wrong way down a one-way street. I guess they changed the directions, but the satnav didn't know that.

**Jack**  So, ⁴_____ , I don't need a new satnav – I just need to update the map.

**Tessa**  Well, to ⁵_____ , that's not the only problem. The display is a bit old-fashioned, too.

**Jack**  Yeah, good ⁶_____ . And the battery isn't very good either, is it?

**Tessa**  No. So really it all adds up to just one thing – buy a new one!

**Jack**  Yeah, ⁷_____ on that. I just haven't got any money right now so it's going to have to wait.

**Tessa**  Yes, ⁸_____ . I spent all my money over the weekend. Well, see you!

## 📖 READING

8  **Read the stories and answer the questions.**

**STORY 1**

1  Why was the woman crying when the police officer arrived?

_____

2  What had the woman and her boyfriend done? Why?

_____

3  How did Officer Meharu know that the burglary was not real?

_____

# THE WORLD'S WORST CRIMINALS?

**1** Recently, police in Calgary, Canada got a call from a woman who said that her home had been burgled. Jewellery was missing, all the home electronics, such as the TV, laptops and tablets, were gone, windows had been smashed, and so on. It isn't surprising that the woman was crying when the police officer arrived. The officer was 37-year-old Charanjit Meharu, who is of Indian origin. While Officer Meharu was checking the crime scene, the woman's phone rang. It was her father, and she began to tell her father – speaking in French – that it wasn't a real burglary: she and her boyfriend had hidden the things, broken the window, and made up the whole story in order to get money from the insurance company. What the woman didn't know is that Officer Meharu speaks seven languages: English, Punjabi, Hindi, Urdu, Arabic, Gujarati – and French!

**2** A few weeks ago a teenager was walking the streets looking for a bike. He found one parked outside a building. There was no one nearby, so he started cutting through the bike lock. He was just about to ride away when a police officer suddenly appeared. The boy hadn't noticed that the building was, in fact, a police station – and that there was a security camera on the wall above the bike! The officer had watched what the boy was doing on the screen inside the building but had let him finish the job first. When he asked him what he was doing, the boy thought for a second, then replied that he was just taking the bike away. He pointed to a sign on the wall that said cyclists weren't allowed to park their bikes there! The police officer smiled but arrested the boy all the same!

**STORY 2**

4  What didn't the boy realise?

_____

5  When did the police officer go out to speak to the boy?

_____

6  Why did the police officer smile?

_____

## ✏️ WRITING

9  **Find another example of a criminal making a stupid mistake and write the story. Write about 150–200 words.**

# 9 IT'S A MYSTERY!

Grammar rap!

## GRAMMAR
### Modals of deduction (present)
→ SB p.86

1  ★☆☆ **Circle the correct options.**

1  They could be Colombian because they're speaking *Spanish / German*.

2  It can't be a spider; it's only got *six / eight* legs.

3  Otis must really love that film. He's seen it *once / ten times*.

4  There can't be anyone at home. All the lights are *on / off*.

5  Jess must travel a lot. Her passport's full of *visa stamps / blank pages*.

6  Bella might be tired. She's been *working hard / doing nothing* all day.

7  They might not speak English. They're *French / American*.

8  Declan must like heavy metal. He *always / never* listens to anything else!

2  ★★☆ **Complete the dialogue with *must / can't / might*.**

**Rachel**  Look, Claudia Woods is on Facebook. I'm going to send her a friend request. There – done.

**Isaac**  Wow, she's got five hundred friends. She ¹_____ be really popular.

**Rachel**  Well, they ²_____ all be real friends. No one can have that many. Not even Claudia.

**Isaac**  That's true. She ³_____ not really know most of them.

**Rachel**  Yes, 20 proper friends at the most. The rest of them ⁴_____ just be friends of friends. She probably just accepts anyone who wants to be her friend.

**Isaac**  Why does she do that?

**Rachel**  I don't know. She ⁵_____ be a bit lonely. Maybe it makes her feel better.

**Isaac**  But that ⁶_____ work. Having lots of false friends doesn't make anyone feel better.

**Rachel**  Oh look. She ⁷_____ be online because she's replied to my request already.

**Isaac**  And what does she say?

**Rachel**  I ⁸_____ believe it. She said no!

## should(n't) have
→ SB p.87

3  ★☆☆ **Complete the sentences with phrases in the list.**

> should invite | shouldn't have gone
> should have invited | should have watched
> shouldn't go | shouldn't have said
> shouldn't say | should watch

1  The documentary last night was brilliant. You _____ it.

2  That old house looks really dangerous. My mum says we _____ inside.

3  You _____ Joe. He'll be upset if you don't.

4  Maxwell _____ anything. It was our secret!

5  We _____ things if we don't really mean them.

6  There's a great film on TV tonight. You _____ it.

7  The party was really boring. We _____ .

8  You _____ Kayla to your party. She was really upset that you didn't.

4  ★★☆ **Read the story and complete the sentences with *should(n't) have* and a verb in the list.**

> charge | go | leave | take | tell | wear

Georgina went on a bike ride. After about 10 km, she had a problem with her bike, but she couldn't fix it because she had no tools with her. She took out her phone, but she couldn't make a call because the phone was out of battery. She decided to get a bus home, but when she looked for her purse, it wasn't in her pocket. There was nothing she could do but walk. It started raining and she got really wet because she didn't have a jacket. Two hours later, when she finally got home, her mum was really angry with her because she had been worried about her. It's the last time Georgina is going on a bike ride without planning it properly.

0  She  *should have taken*  some tools with her.

1  She _____ her phone before leaving.

2  She _____ her purse at home.

3  She _____ a jacket.

4  She _____ her mum where she was going.

5  She _____ on a bike ride without planning it properly!

**5** ★★★ **Complete the conversations with your own ideas. Use should(n't) have.**

0  **A** I'm so tired today.
   *You should have gone to bed earlier.*
1  **A** This T-shirt is too small for me.
   **B** _____
2  **A** Jake's really angry with me.
   **B** _____
3  **A** I'm so thirsty, but I haven't got anything to drink.
   **B** _____
4  **A** I haven't got enough money left to get the bus.
   **B** _____
5  **A** I don't understand this homework at all.
   **B** _____

## Modals of deduction (past)  → SB p.89

**6** ★☆☆ **Match the parts of the sentences.**

1  Peter crashed Nicola's scooter again. ☐
2  Liam ate everything. ☐
3  But he was too polite to ask for some food. ☐
4  Rosa's football team won the cup. ☐
5  Andy didn't eat anything. ☐
6  But it's always difficult to know what she's feeling. ☐

a  She must have been happy.
b  She can't have been happy.
c  Nadia might have been happy.
d  He must have been hungry.
e  He can't have been hungry.
f  He could have been hungry.

**7** ★★☆ **Complete the text with the verbs in brackets and the correct modal verbs.**

Police are still looking for the multi-millionaire banker Cecil Montgomery who disappeared from his home last week. At first, they were sure criminals ¹_____ (take) him from the family home, but now they are investigating the possibility that he ²_____ (disappear) on purpose. It seems that he was having financial problems and owed a lot of people a lot of money and police believe that he ³_____ (go) into hiding to escape from these people. One thing we know for sure is that he ⁴_____ (leave) the country as police found his passport in his office desk. Police are now asking members of the public for their help. They feel certain that someone ⁵_____ (see) Cecil in the last few days and they are asking that person to come forward and help them with their investigation.

**8** ★★★ **Complete the sentences with your own ideas. Use modals of deduction.**

1  Our headteacher looks really happy. She _____
   _____
2  I recognise his face. I'm sure _____
   _____
3  Nobody went to their party. They _____
   _____
4  I'm not sure how I fell off my bike. I _____
   _____
5  Our cat is missing. I'm worried _____
   _____
6  Josie is two hours late – _____
   _____
7  The baby fell asleep in two minutes – _____
   _____
8  Perry hasn't got any money – _____
   _____

## GET IT RIGHT!

### Modals of deduction: past

**Learners sometimes use *can have* for speculating about past events when *could have* is needed. But remember, we use *can't have* in the negative.**

✓ He could have known the truth.
✗ He can have known the truth.
✓ He can't have known the truth.

**Choose the correct sentence in each pair.**

1  a  It must be in the garage. It can have been put anywhere else.
   b  It must be in the garage. It can't have been put anywhere else.
2  a  Do you think it could have been someone else?
   b  Do you think it can have been someone else?
3  a  She can't have known about it because nobody told her.
   b  She could have known about it because nobody told her.
4  a  I don't think we can have managed it without your help.
   b  I don't think we could have managed it without your help.
5  a  They can't have got there in time. Their car was too slow.
   b  They could have got there in time. Their car was too slow.

# VOCABULARY
## Mysteries

→ SB p.86

**1** ★☆☆ **Find eight words about mysteries in the wordsearch.**

| N | T | E | R | O | F | E | A | K | R | I | O | W | S | M | O |
|---|---|---|---|---|---|---|---|---|---|---|---|---|---|---|---|
| K | B | P | U | Z | Z | L | I | N | G | A | W | U | U | J | T |
| N | O | X | H | P | S | H | Z | Z | V | Q | U | E | O | G | R |
| E | X | T | R | A | T | E | R | R | E | S | T | R | I | A | L |
| I | H | E | A | N | R | P | A | R | I | E | O | Y | R | E | R |
| L | A | I | A | N | A | O | D | D | A | C | B | D | E | A | N |
| A | I | L | V | O | N | T | R | M | O | R | U | I | T | E | S |
| W | K | N | A | R | G | F | E | W | D | E | X | W | S | R | Y |
| T | L | E | A | T | E | A | S | P | C | T | B | E | Y | H | F |
| S | E | U | N | E | X | P | L | A | I | N | E | D | M | T | Y |

1 _____
2 _____
3 _____
4 _____
5 _____
6 _____
7 _____
8 _____

**2** ★★☆ **Circle the correct words.**

1 Hannah hasn't returned my call, which is really *strange / unexplained*.
2 I didn't really understand the end of the film. It was a bit *secret / puzzling*.
3 Scientists believe the object is *odd / alien* and from another planet.
4 I don't want you to tell anyone. It's top *puzzling / secret*.
5 Paul's behaviour is a bit *alien / mysterious*. I think he might have a secret!
6 I'm sure I had a £10 note in my wallet but it isn't here. That's *secret / odd*.
7 I didn't like that man. He was very *extraterrestrial / strange*.
8 To this day, the disappearance of our neighbour is still *alien / unexplained*.

## Expressions with *go*

→ SB p.89

**3** ★☆☆ **Match the sentences or the parts of the sentences.**

1 I don't think the party's ☐
2 We've set the dates so now we need to go one step further and ☐
3 We had a great time at the concert. ☐
4 I think it goes without saying ☐
5 The film was so slow and boring and ☐
6 That funny video clip ☐

a We all went crazy when they played our favourite song!
b it went on for hours.
c has gone viral!
d decide where to go!
e going very well.
f that you aren't coming in here.

**4** ★★☆ **Complete the conversations with the expressions in the list.**

> crazy | for | on | one step further
> really well | up | viral | without saying

1 **A** How much are the cinema tickets?
  **B** £12. They've gone _____ recently. They were £9.
2 **A** Your sister likes dancing, doesn't she?
  **B** Likes?! She goes _____ when she gets the chance to dance!
3 **A** How was the exam?
  **B** It went _____ . I think I've passed.
4 **A** Do you want to try again to lift 100 kg?
  **B** I think I'll go _____ and try 110 kg.
5 **A** Why are you so late?
  **B** Sorry. My music lesson went _____ longer than usual.
6 **A** Did you watch that video clip I posted?
  **B** Yes. It's amazing. It went _____ immediately!
7 **A** Have you decided what to have?
  **B** I think I'll go _____ the vegetable curry, please.
8 **A** So are you going to invite me to your party?
  **B** Of course – it goes _____ . You are my best friend, after all.

84

# REFERENCE

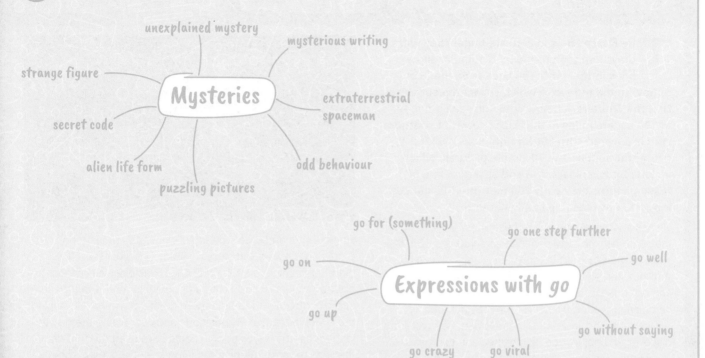

## VOCABULARY *EXTRA*

**1 Match the words (1–7) with the definitions (a–g).**

1 astonished ☐
2 confused ☐
3 invisible ☐
4 frightened ☐
5 magic ☐
6 suspicious ☐
7 weird ☐

a scared
b having special powers
c feeling something is wrong
d very surprised
e strange or odd
f unable to understand
g impossible to see

**2 Complete the table with the words in Exercise 1.**

| Words to describe people, things or situations | Words to describe how people feel |
|---|---|
| _____ | _____ |
| _____ | _____ |
| _____ | _____ |
| _____ | _____ |

**3 Circle the correct words.**

1 The text was so small that it was almost *weird / invisible*.
2 We were *astonished / frightened* when our project won the prize.
3 I didn't feel happy about going into the cave. In fact, I was *weird / frightened*.
4 The explanation wasn't clear and we were all *invisible / confused*.
5 Some of the paintings were unusual and others were totally *invisible / weird*.
6 The message didn't make sense and I began to feel *magic / suspicious* that something wasn't right.
7 It comes on automatically – it's like *astonished / magic*!

**4 Complete the sentences about your own experiences.**

1 I felt confused when _____
_____

2 I was astonished when _____
_____

3 I felt frightened when _____
_____

4 I was suspicious when _____
_____

# THE NAZCA LINES OF PERU

The Nazca Lines in Peru are huge! They were drawn on the ground by digging shallow lines in the earth. The lines were made by removing the red stone which covers the surface so that the white rock below could be seen. An area of 190 square miles in the Nazca desert in southern Peru is covered with 800 straight lines, 300 geometric shapes and 70 simple pictures, which include birds, spiders, fish and sharks. Some of these pictures are nearly 200 metres wide and the longest lines reach up to 48 kilometres.

What's so mysterious about these lines? Well, although they date back to between the years 400 and 650, they were only discovered in the 1930s. The reason is that the lines and pictures are invisible from the ground and can only be seen from the air. It was only when aeroplanes started flying over the area that people realised that the lines were there. When they were first discovered, people were astonished and confused. Of course, this led to the question: how did these pictures get there all those years ago? Surely they can't have been made without modern tools. People didn't have the ability to fly so long ago. Or did they? Author Jim Woodman suggested that the Nazca people could have invented simple hot-air balloons and used them to produce the art. He even built a working balloon using the same materials they would have used. Not many people were convinced by his ideas though. Other people suggested the lines might be extraterrestrial and that they were the work of aliens visiting Earth. More and more theories were offered and one of the great modern mysteries was created.

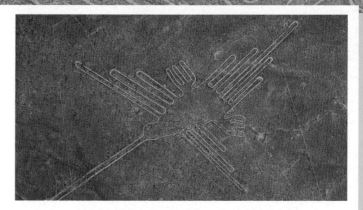

However, when some wooden sticks were found in the ground in the area and carbon-dated, it showed that they were the same age as the drawings. This discovery made scientists wonder if the Nazca people might have put these sticks in the ground to help them do the drawings. By placing the sticks in the correct positions and connecting them with long ropes, the Nazca people could have used them to draw the lines to make the pictures. One scientist, Dr Joe Nickell of the University of Kentucky, was so sure that this was the answer that he decided to try and show how it could be done. Using only the tools that the Nazca people might have had, he set about trying to draw a huge picture of a bird on a piece of land. With the help of several friends, it took him only a few hours to produce a perfect Nazca picture and to show at long last how these pictures probably got there.

Among the mysteries of the Nazca Lines, there is one clear fact. The lines and pictures can still be seen after around 1,500 years because of the climate. They are in a desert with very little wind and less than 2.5 cm of rain a year. This explains why the lines are in such good condition today.

## READING

1  **Read the article and choose the correct option.**

The Nazca Lines were made …

A  over a thousand years ago.

B  nearly 100 years ago.

C  recently.

2  **Read the article again and answer the questions.**

1  How were the lines drawn?

_____

2  What invention led to the discovery of the Nazca Lines? Why?

_____

3  What did Jim Woodman make?

_____

4  What discovery gave Dr Joe Nickell the idea for his theory?

_____

5  Why can we still see the Nazca Lines today?

_____

3  CRITICAL THINKING  **Find evidence in the text that supports the theories about the Nazca Lines.**

1  The Nazca people could fly.

_____

2  The Nazca Lines were made by aliens.

_____

3  The Nazca Lines were made using simple tools.

_____

4  **Answer the question with your own ideas.**

What do you think? How were the Nazca Lines made?

_____

_____

_____

PRONUNCIATION

Moving word stress  Go to page 120.

# DEVELOPING *Writing*

## A blog entry explaining a mystery

**1** **INPUT** **Read the blog and answer the questions.**

1 What is the mystery?

_____

2 When and where did it happen?

_____

3 Has it been solved?

_____

---

BLOG | ABOUT | NEWS | ARCHIVES | CONTACT ME 🔍

# What happened to Flight MH370?

**Malaysian Airlines Flight MH370 took off from Kuala Lumpur airport in Malaysia on 8 March 2014. Forty minutes later, it had disappeared. Nothing has been heard of the plane or its 227 passengers and 12 crew since then, despite the biggest search in the history of air travel.**

The disappearance of Flight MH370 is unexplained, and people have come up with their own theories about what happened.

One suggestion is that the plane might have caught fire and crashed into the sea. In fact, it was carrying over 200 kg of lithium batteries, which explode very easily.

A sudden loss of air pressure in the cabin would have killed everyone, including the pilots, and caused a crash. However, someone suggested the co-pilot alone survived and could have flown the plane until it crashed. ¹_____ .

In a book about the mystery, a historian claims the plane must have vanished as the result of a remote cyber hijacking because it had important material or people onboard. Surely that can't be true!

²_____ people on social media liked the theory of another Bermuda Triangle in the Indian Ocean. They believe Flight MH370 must have disappeared in the same place where other planes had vanished before. ³_____

Some people even believe the plane was hijacked by aliens, ⁴_____ .

The most likely explanation is that there must have been a problem with the plane – ⁵_____ . Cracks had been found in other Boeing 777s which could have caused the plane to break up.

⁶_____

---

**2** **ANALYSE** **Blogs are usually informal in style. Complete the gaps (1–6) with the phrases (a–f). Sometimes there is more than one correct answer.**

a but I'm not a big believer in extraterrestrials
b but why?
c That's one of the weirdest things I've ever heard!
d That's what I think.
e What do you think really happened to Flight MH370?
f Millions of

**3** **Match the phrases in Exercise 2 (a–f) with their functions (1–6).**

1 giving your own opinion ☐
2 explaining your opinion ☐
3 inviting other opinions ☐
4 using a superlative to say you don't believe it ☐
5 exaggeration ☐
6 responding to an unexplained theory ☐

**4** **When trying to explain a mystery, we use modal verbs of deduction and conditionals. <u>Underline</u> all the examples of these forms in the article.**

**5** **PLAN** **Do some research into a mystery in your country and make a plan. Make sure you include all the points below.**

- the facts • possible explanations • your opinion

**6** **PRODUCE** **Write your blog entry (200 words). Use some of the phrases in Exercise 2 and your plan from Exercise 5. Make sure you include all the points from the checklist.**

 **CHECKLIST**

Use an informal style.
Use modal verbs of deduction and conditionals to suggest explanations.
Include your own opinions.
Invite your readers to comment.

 **LISTENING**

**1** 🔊 9.03 **Listen to two dialogues. Match the sentences (a–d) to the dialogues (1–2)**

  a  Someone made a mistake. ☐

  b  Someone lost something. ☐

  c  The speakers are getting ready to travel. ☐

  d  The speakers are waiting for someone. ☐

**2** 🔊 9.03 **Listen again and choose the correct answers.**

  **1**

  a  Eddie thinks the missing thing is *certainly* / *probably* in his room.

  b  His mum *advises* / *warns* him what to do with important things.

  c  They set off *earlier* / *later* than planned.

  **2**

  a  Dylan *is* / *isn't* surprised that Jess isn't there.

  b  Dylan thinks it is *possible* / *impossible* that Jess has forgotten.

  c  Jess *must* / *can't* have understood the plan they'd made.

**3** 🔊 9.03 **Complete these parts of the dialogues with *should(n't) have* and a verb in the list. Then listen and check.**

> go | keep | rush | tell

  **1**

**Eddie**  I must have put it in a safe place, but I can't remember where.

**Mum**  You ¹_____ it with your other important things, like your wallet and phone.

**Mum**  OK, so, when did you last have it?

**Eddie**  Last night! I had it in my hand, I remember. Ah, I ²_____ so much!

  **2**

**Tanya**  You ³_____ her to be here at seven – you know she's always late.

**Dylan**  You're right, but she should be here by now.

**Dylan**  You won't believe it! She's waiting for us outside the café.

**Tanya**  She ⁴_____ there! We're going there after the film.

## DIALOGUE

**4** **Put the missing lines in the correct places to make three short dialogues.**

  **1**

**Lewis**  Have you seen the TV remote, Adam?

**Adam**  _____

**Lewis**  _____

**Adam**  _____

**Lewis**  _____

  **2**

**Beth**  Any news from the police on the missing Picasso painting?

**Fraser**  _____

**Beth**  _____

**Fraser**  _____

**Beth**  _____

  **3**

**Polly**  My bike. Someone's stolen it!

**Chris**  _____

**Polly**  _____

**Chris**  _____

**Polly**  _____

  1  So try the dog basket – Spike might have taken it.

  2  Stolen it. Are you sure?

  3  Well, it was long enough for them to break the lock. I don't believe it!

  4  Well, let's hope they arrest someone soon and find the painting.

  5  I think it must have been someone who worked at the gallery.

  6  Of course I'm sure. I left it locked up just here.

  7  That's a good idea. I'll go and have a look.

  8  No, I haven't. It's probably down the side of the sofa. That's where it usually is.

  9  They can't have gone far – we were only in the shop for five minutes.

  10  I've already searched the whole sofa. It isn't there.

  11  No, they don't even know how the robber got into the building.

  12  Yes, I think you're right. Someone who knew how to turn off the alarm.

**5** **Use one of the lines below to start or end a five-line dialogue.**

  1  You shouldn't have done that!

  2  You should have told me straightaway.

  3  It must have been my sister.

  4  It can't have been easy.

# TOWARDS B2 First for Schools

## LISTENING
### Sentence completion

### EXAM GUIDE

You will listen to a monologue, such as a talk, a presentation or part of a radio programme. While you are listening, you have to complete ten sentences using the information you hear in the recording.

Before you listen …

- read the title and the text as these will prepare you for what you are going to hear.
- look carefully at the words **before** and **after** the gaps.
- think about the type of information you need to complete each sentence.
- underline the key words.

While you listen …

- remember the questions follow the same order as the recording.
- you must only write **one**, **two** or **three** words in each gap.
- focus carefully on the details.
- you will hear the **exact word(s)** you need to complete the gaps in the recording.
- read the completed sentences to make sure they make sense.

1  🔊 9.04  **You will hear Gaby talking about an unforgettable school trip to the ancient monument of Stonehenge in south-west England. For questions 1–10, complete the sentences with a word or short phrase.**

## ——————————— SCHOOL TRIP ———————————

The visit to Stonehenge was the ¹_____ of Gaby's trip to the UK.

The first thing that impressed her about Stonehenge was its ²_____ .

It's estimated that work started on Stonehenge about ³_____ years ago.

The stones that were used in the ⁴_____ of construction came from mountains in Wales.

The biggest stones were so heavy that they must have been ⁵_____ there on tree trunks.

Gaby says Stonehenge is ⁶_____ other ancient monuments because the reason it was built is still a mystery.

People come here to see the ⁷_____ on the longest and shortest days of the year.

It might have been used for observing ⁸_____ of stars in the night sky.

Another theory is that it was a type of ⁹_____ that showed the passing hours by the position of the sunlight on the stones.

Gaby doesn't believe the monument was constructed by ¹⁰_____ .

# 10 MONEY

## GRAMMAR
### Future continuous
→ SB p.94

1 ★☆☆ **Put the words in order to make sentences. Use the future continuous.**

This time next year, …

0 my / present / cookery show / grandma / on TV / a
*My grandma will be presenting a cookery show on TV.*

1 dad / my / race / the / in / Grand Prix
_____
_____

2 sister / work / children's home / Cambodia / in / my / at / a
_____
_____

3 brother / my / sail / world / the / around
_____
_____

4 mum / act / my / in / a / production / theatre
_____
_____

5 cousin / research / my / cancer / cure / a / for
_____
_____

6 best friend / trek / Africa / round / my
_____
_____

7 I / human rights / a / lawyer / famous / work / as
_____
_____

2 ★★★ **What do you think will be happening 50 years from now? Use the ideas in brackets to write sentences in the future continuous.**

0 (type of transport / travel)
*People will be travelling in computer-controlled flying cars.*

1 (phones / use)
_____

2 (money / use)
_____

3 (school textbooks / use)
_____

4 (houses / live)
_____

3 ★★★ **Write fantasy predictions for your friends and family. Use the future continuous.**

Ten years from now, …

1 my _____
_____

2 my _____
_____

3 my _____
_____

4 my _____
_____

5 my _____
_____

6 I _____
_____

### Future perfect
→ SB p.97

4 ★☆☆ **Complete the conversation with the future perfect tense of the verbs in brackets.**

**Mum** Have you done your homework yet?

**Kyle** No, but I [1]_____ (finish) it by the time Dad gets home.

**Mum** Have you tidied your room yet?

**Kyle** No, but I [2]_____ (tidy) it by bedtime.

**Mum** Have you fed the cat yet?

**Kyle** No, but I [3]_____ (feed) it by 6 pm.

**Mum** Have you done that essay yet?

**Kyle** No, but I [4]_____ (write) it by this time tomorrow.

**Mum** And have you prepared dinner yet?

**Kyle** No, but I [5]_____ (make) it by the time everyone gets hungry.

5  ★★☆  **Complete the conversation with the future perfect of the verbs in the list.**

> become | buy | cycle | find
> finish | go | move | not have
> sail | see | swim | travel

**Yuri**   What plans have you got for the future, Penny?

**Penny**   Me? By 2030, I ¹_____ university, and I ²_____ to New York. I ³_____ an amazing apartment there, and I ⁴_____ a successful architect.

**Yuri**   Wow!

**Penny**   What about you? ⁵_____ you _____ round the world? You always said you'd like to do that.

**Yuri**   Of course. I ⁶_____ across the English Channel, and I ⁷_____ across the Atlantic Ocean. I ⁸_____ across China, and I ⁹_____ the pyramids in Mexico and Guatemala. Oh, and of course, I ¹⁰_____ kayaking down the Grand Canyon.

**Penny**   ¹¹_____ a job?

**Yuri**   No, I ¹²_____ time to find a job!

## Future perfect and future continuous

6  ★★☆  **Complete the predictions with the future perfect or the future continuous.**

1  By 2030, internet use _____ (reach) 7.5 billion worldwide.
2  By 2040, smoking in public _____ (be) banned in every US state.
3  By 2050, robots _____ (work) in factories instead of humans.
4  By 2060, people _____ (use) telepathy to communicate.
5  By 2070, nearly half the Amazon rainforest _____ (be) cut down.
6  By 2080, scientists_____ (invent) invisibility suits.
7  By 2090, people _____ (drive) flying cars.
8  By 2100, many of the world's languages _____ (disappear).

7  ★★☆  **Complete the text with the future perfect or the future continuous of the verbs in the list.**

> become | build | eat | explore
> live | produce | ~~travel~~

By 2050, I don't think people ⁰ *will have travelled* to Mars. However, I think they ¹_____ space. Some people ²_____ in space stations, because the Earth ³_____ too crowded.
I think scientists ⁴_____ huge farms in space in special glass buildings, and they ⁵_____ very healthy food for everyone.
People ⁶_____ specially developed fruit and vegetables.

8  ★★★  **Write goals for yourself. Complete the sentences using the future perfect or future continuous.**

1  By tomorrow evening, I _____ _____
2  By next week, _____ _____
3  By next year, _____ _____
4  By the time I'm 20, _____ _____
5  By the time I'm 50, _____ _____

## GET IT RIGHT!

### Future perfect vs. future simple

Learners often confuse the future perfect with the future simple.

✓  *By the end of next year, I will have finished my studies.*
✗  *By the end of next year, I will finish my studies.*

**Complete the sentences with the verb in brackets in the correct form: future perfect or future simple.**

0  I *will have gone back* to Beijing by June. (go)
1  We hope you _____ to our party next weekend. (come)
2  I'd really like that game – maybe my parents _____ it for my birthday. (buy)
3  By the time I finish my English course, my skills _____ a lot. (improve)
4  I promise I _____ there at 5 pm tomorrow. (be)
5  We hope that in a week's time we _____ all our exams! (finish)
6  By this time tomorrow, they _____ in Australia. (arrive)

# VOCABULARY
## Money and value

→ SB p.94

1 ★★☆ **Complete the sentences with the words and phrases in the list. There are three you don't need.**

> bargain | refund | off | offer
> owe | reward | tip | valuable
> value for money | worth

1 This ruby ring is quite _____ .
My great-grandmother gave it to my mum.
2 My grandad's stamp collection is
_____ a lot of money now.
3 I _____ Jack some money. I borrowed
£10 from him last week.
4 These trainers are usually over £50. I got them for
£20. They were a real _____ .
5 We got the tent for half price. I think it's very good
_____ .
6 The shop owner gave me a _____
for catching the shoplifter.
7 There's a winter sale at the sports shop – £10
_____ everything!

2 ★☆☆ **Complete the dialogue with some of the words and phrases in Exercise 1.**

**Felix** Is that a new bike you've got there?

**Leonie** Yeah! It's really cool and I only paid £100 for it.

**Felix** £100! That's a ¹_____ .
It's ²_____ a lot more than that.

**Leonie** Yes, it was on ³_____ – £75
⁴_____ in the sale.

**Felix** That's great ⁵_____ money.

**Leonie** The only problem is I now ⁶_____
my parents £50. I only had £50 in savings,
so they lent me the rest of the money.

## Jobs and work

→ SB p.97

3 ★☆☆ **Circle the correct words.**

1 My dad works in *healthcare / finance*. He's a nurse.
2 What *management / qualifications* do you need to
be an air traffic controller?
3 I've been an *employee / employer* of SmartArt for
ten years now.
4 Ms Brown is my *employer / employee*. I've worked
for her company for 15 years now.
5 Peter's got a *finance / management* job now –
he's got a team of people working under him.
6 She does scientific experiments for the government;
she works in *finance / public service*.

4 ★★☆ **Match the sentences.**

1 I'm a bank employee. ☐
2 I work as a consultant in a hospital. ☐
3 I am a headteacher at a primary school
in North London. ☐
4 I've got a job in a government office. ☐
5 I want to be a High Court judge. ☐

a I work in education.
b I work in public services.
c I work in finance.
d I'm studying Law at university.
e I work in healthcare.

## WordWise: Phrases with *by*

→ SB p.95

5 **Read the four sentences. In which sentence is
*by* used …**

1 to say how something is done? ☐
2 to say where something is? ☐
3 to say when something is/will be done? ☐
4 to say who does something? ☐

a There's no traffic today, so I think we'll get
there by nine o'clock.
b I bought these shoes at that new shop by
the supermarket.
c This photo was taken by my grandmother.
d I bought my new computer by saving up for
six months!

6 **Complete the sentences.**

> by working | by a friend | by ten o'clock
> by my bedroom door | by Monday
> by practising

1 This book was written _____ of
my teacher's.
2 We've got three days to do the
homework – the teacher said he wants it
_____ .
3 I learned to play the guitar
_____ for two hours every day.
4 James made some money _____
in a café at the weekends.
5 Our cat always sleeps _____ .
6 The film starts at 8 pm, so I'm sure it will have
finished _____ .

# REFERENCE

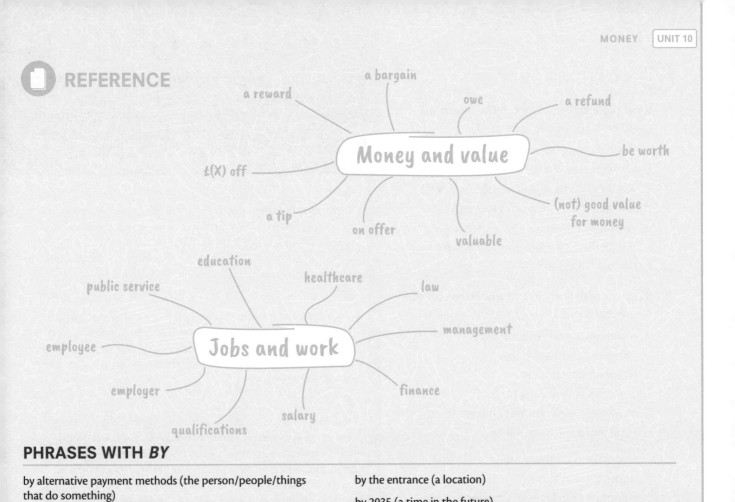

**Money and value**
- a bargain
- a reward
- owe
- a refund
- be worth
- £(X) off
- (not) good value for money
- a tip
- on offer
- valuable

**Jobs and work**
- education
- healthcare
- law
- public service
- management
- employee
- finance
- employer
- salary
- qualifications

## PHRASES WITH *BY*

by alternative payment methods (the person/people/things that do something)

by answering (a way to do something)

by the entrance (a location)

by 2035 (a time in the future)

# VOCABULARY *EXTRA*

**1 Match the words and phrases in the list to their meanings.**

be in credit | debt | grant | loan | payment | savings

1 money given by an organisation for a special purpose, e.g. to study a course _____

2 an amount of money you spend for a particular thing _____

3 an amount of money you borrow, often from a bank _____

4 having money available in your bank account _____

5 money you don't spend, but keep for later _____

6 money that you owe someone _____

**2 Complete the sentences with the words and phrases in Exercise 1.**

1 My sister received a _____ to study at university.

2 I'm going to use my _____ to go on a holiday with my friends.

3 Matthew owed me £20 but he paid off his _____ when he got his wages.

4 My mum made the _____ for the tickets by credit card.

5 My parents got a _____ from the bank to buy our flat.

6 Now Kieran's got a job, his bank account _____ .

**3 Answer the questions with your own ideas.**

1 Do students get grants in your country?

_____

_____

_____

2 In your country, which types of payment are most popular?

_____

_____

_____

3 Do you think it's important to pay off debts as soon as you can?

_____

_____

_____

4 Do you think it's important to have savings? Why?

_____

_____

_____

**1** Read the article and match the questions (a–g) with the paragraphs (1–7).

a What are the advantages?

b What are community currencies exactly?

c Are they the same as national currency?

d Are community currencies successful?

e Why does a town need its own money?

f What's the future for community currencies?

g How do they work?

**2** Read the article again and match the parts of the sentences.

1 A community currency belongs ☐

2 The main advantage is that ☐

3 Businesses can decide ☐

4 Community currencies make ☐

5 Most community currency projects ☐

6 Local money projects will be ☐

a to join the project or not.

b work very well.

c it improves the financial situation.

d expanding over the next few years.

e to a single town or area.

f people's lives better in many ways.

**3** CRITICAL THINKING Read the article again and match a possible disadvantage to Paragraph 1–6. Can you think of any other disadvantages?

Paragraph 1 ☐   Paragraph 4 ☐

Paragraph 2 ☐   Paragraph 5 ☐

Paragraph 3 ☐   Paragraph 6 ☐

a People might prefer to pay by cash in local shops.

b It can't be used everywhere.

c You can't use the money for saving.

d It doesn't help the national economy.

e You have less choice if you only buy local products.

f Not all shops and businesses accept the local money.

# LOCAL MONEY £ $

The dollar, pound, euro, peso and real are well-known world currencies, but have you heard of the Bristol Pound, the Abeille or the Urstromtaler? Probably not, because these currencies are only used in single towns. They are all examples of community currencies.

**1** _____ ?

A community currency is money that can only be spent in one particular place. It doesn't replace the national currency – it is used as an alternative instead. For example, in the city of Bristol in the UK, people can pay for their shopping in pounds sterling (£) or in Bristol pounds (£B).

**2** _____ ?

The aim of a community currency is to help the town's economy. It encourages residents to support businesses in the area so that the money stays in the local community. In this way, businesses grow, attract new customers and create new jobs, which makes the economy stronger.

**3** _____ ?

First, the town has to set up a community interest company. This company holds a sum of national currency and prints banknotes in the community currency. Businesses join the project by agreeing to accept these banknotes as payment from customers. People who are paid in local money or get it as change can spend it in the shops and businesses which are part of the project.

**4** _____ ?

There's one important difference between national and local money: local banknotes have a spend-by date printed on them and if the banknotes aren't spent before this date, they become worthless. Community currencies work better if the money is being used actively rather than saved.

**5** _____ ?

Towns which have tried this experiment have found lots of benefits. Having their own currency brings the community together, which creates a positive identity. People who are proud of their town get involved in new projects, such as organising events and charity work. Thinking locally is not only good for the economy, but also for the environment. By buying local products, you save energy and reduce pollution. The local currency also helps local shops compete against the multinationals by encouraging people to buy from them instead of from big supermarkets and chains.

**6** _____ ?

The numbers speak for themselves: in Bristol, over £B 5 million were spent in the first six years of the project. Bristol's residents can pay for public transport, services, shopping and even local taxes using community money. There are over 10,000 community currencies around the world, and more are being planned.

**7** _____ ?

The world is moving towards a cashless society. It is predicted that banknotes and coins will have disappeared before the end of the century in many countries. Community currencies will be playing an important part in the cashless world. Community interest companies have been following current trends by creating mobile apps for digital payments. Experts are hoping that this user-friendly, cheap technology will soon be helping communities in the developing world to create community currencies which will bring them the benefits they need.

# DEVELOPING Writing

## An essay

1 **INPUT** Read Ava's essay. Circle the correct options.

1 Overall, Ava thinks the statement in the title is *true* / *false*.

2 When Ava writes 'I really envy them', she's *agreeing* / *disagreeing* with the title.

3 When Ava writes 'I'd rather go camping …' , she's *agreeing* / *disagreeing* with the title.

### Time to enjoy life is more important than earning a lot of money

Both my parents have successful careers in the finance industry and are very well paid, but they're hardly ever at home. They earn a lot of money, but they don't have much time to enjoy life. My friend Grace's family don't have as much money as us, but they have a lot of fun doing things together. I really envy them.

Firstly, people who have high salaries often don't have time to spend their money because they are working all the time. **Secondly**, they spend more time at work than with their families and they don't have much energy for free-time activities either.

When my mum and dad are at home, they're so tired they just relax.

**Without doubt**, a good salary gives you security because you don't have any money worries. You are able to buy everything you and your family need. In addition, you have probably reached the top of your career and your job is interesting and gives you a lot of satisfaction. But will you be happy? What's more, will your family be happy?

On the one hand, money makes you wealthy but on the other, it makes you time-poor. My parents can take us on fantastic holidays and give us treats. **However**, they can't give us the time we would like with them. I'd rather go on camping trips in the school holidays like Grace's family. **For these reasons**, I believe that a high salary is definitely not as important as having time to spend with your family.

2 **Match the words in bold in the essay with the words with similar meanings (1–4). Then find three other linking words or phrases in the essay.**

a but     1 _____

b furthermore     2 _____

c therefore     3 _____

d without question     4 _____

_____ , _____ , _____

3 **ANALYSE** **Put the statements in order to make Ava's essay plan.**

☐ a conclusion

☐ b introduction stating my opinion

☐ c the first argument against the statement

☐ d the first argument for the statement

☐ e the second argument against the statement

☐ f the second argument for the statement

4 **Look at the text again and <u>underline</u> the examples Ava gives to support her ideas.**

5 **PLAN** **You are going to write an essay with the title:** *Money isn't the most important thing in the world.* **Complete the plan with your ideas.**

| | |
|---|---|
| Introduction | |
| Arguments for the statement | |
| Arguments against the statement | |
| Conclusion | |

6 **PRODUCE**  **Write your essay (200–250 words). Use your plan from Exercise 5. Make sure you include all the points in the checklist.**

### ✓ CHECKLIST

Write in a formal style.

Organise your essay into paragraphs.

Use linking words to join your ideas.

Give examples to support your ideas.

## 🎧 LISTENING

1 🔊 10.01 **Listen to the dialogue between Libby and Brad. Match the plans (a–d) with the people.**

Libby ☐ ☐          Brad ☐ ☐

a do a sports course       c improve a skill
b go to a concert          d look for a job

2 🔊 10.01 **Listen again and mark the sentences T (true) or F (false). Then correct the false sentences.**

1 Libby couldn't go away with her friends because she had to work. ☐

2 She has started saving her money for a future event. ☐

3 Brad's going to the music festival with Louis. ☐

4 Brad will probably do the same summer job as last year. ☐

5 Libby's parents hope she'll become a professional dancer. ☐

6 Libby's certain her parents will let her go to France if she gets a place on the course. ☐

## DIALOGUE

3 🔊 10.01 **Listen again and complete these parts of the dialogue.**

**Brad** Are you alone?

**Libby** Yeah, my friends all are at the music festival. I ¹_____ customers at the café all day tomorrow while they ²_____ and enjoying the festival.

**Brad** ³_____ ! Why didn't you go with them?

**Libby** I didn't have enough money for the ticket.

**Brad** ⁴_____ , you can go next year.

**Brad** OK, I suppose it isn't that bad. You get fit and you can earn a lot if you work at weekends. Maybe I'll just do that because if I don't earn some money, I ⁵_____ and then I won't be able to go on holiday with my friends.

**Libby** Wow! Without your parents?

**Brad** Yes, first time! We'll be spending the last week of August camping at the seaside.

**Libby** Lucky you!

**Brad** The place has got a surf school and by the end of the week, we ⁶_____ to surf – with a bit of luck!

**Libby** Cool! I wish I was doing something exciting this summer. I wanted to go to a summer school in France, but I ⁷_____ now.

**Brad** ⁸_____ !

## PHRASES FOR FLUENCY  → SB p.98

4 **Complete the phrases. Then match them with the phrases which are similar.**

1 s_m_ _s _s_ _l ☐
2 D_n't l_ _k _t m_! ☐
3 _'m br_ke ☐
4 _r_ _n m_ ☐
5 th_t's _ll ☐
6 _t's n_t my f_ _lt ☐

a I have no money.
b I didn't do it!
c There's no difference.
d I will pay for them!
e Someone else did it!
f I only meant …

5 **Now complete the dialogues with some of the phrases in Exercise 4.**

1
**A** Hi, Joe. You seem really busy these days. I haven't seen you around!
**B** Oh, it's the ¹_____ . Too much to do and not enough time!
**A** Well, tell me if you want to hang out.
**B** No, not today, sorry.
**A** Sure, I was worried about you, ²_____ .

2
**A** Are you coming for an ice cream?
**B** I can't. ³_____ .
**A** Don't worry. The ice-creams ⁴_____ . My grandad gave me some money for cutting the grass in his garden.
**B** Cool! Thanks!

3
**A** What's happened to my phone? The screen's smashed!
**B** ⁵_____ ! A girl walked by and her bag knocked it onto the floor.
**A** But you should have moved it for me!
**B** ⁶_____ ! You shouldn't have left it on the edge of the table!

**PRONUNCIATION**
Short and long vowel sounds: $/ɪ/$ – $/iː/$ and $/ɒ/$ – $/əʊ/$ **Go to page 121.** 🎧

 **WRITING**
An essay

## EXAM GUIDE

For this part of the test, you have to write an essay. You are given the title of the essay and some notes to use. Two of the notes are already completed, but you have to think of an idea for the third note.

- Read the question and the notes carefully.
- Write a short plan.
- Organise your essay into paragraphs.
- You have about 40 minutes to write your answer to Part 1.

In Justin's English class, they have been discussing education. Their teacher has asked them to write an essay for homework.

Write your essay using all the notes and giving reasons for your point of view.

Write 140–190 words.

> **Secondary schools should offer vocational courses – courses that train you for a job.**
>
> **Notes**
>
> Write about:
> 1  skills for work
> 2  benefits of university
> 3  _____ (your own idea)

1  Read Justin's notes (a–f) for his essay. Which point, 1 or 2, in the essay question does each note belong to?

> ### Secondary schools should offer vocational courses
>
> Most schools prepare students for university, but they don't prepare them for a job.
> However, there are many school-leavers who decide to start work straightaway. These students would benefit from vocational courses which give them practical qualifications.
> These courses should be offered as an alternative to academic lessons. Firstly, many students prefer practical work to studying. Vocational courses would motivate them to work harder.
> Most importantly, they are good for students who find it hard to study and sit quietly in class. However, vocational courses are often difficult for schools to organise because they need special teachers and expensive equipment.
> Students who enjoy studying should still try for university. Parents often believe that a degree leads to a better job. University prepares young people for life by giving them opportunities to meet different people and try new experiences. University isn't for everybody. There are other interesting careers that don't require a degree.
> Therefore, I think vocational courses should be included in the school curriculum.

a  suitable for students who prefer learning practical skills – not studying ☐

b  good for students who like studying ☐

c  can learn about different jobs, for example: computer programming, hairdressing ☐

d  learn a useful skill for work ☐

e  an experience that prepares you for the future in many ways ☐

f  adults think a university degree gives more opportunities for a career ☐

2  Read Justin's essay again. What is his own idea for point 3?

3  Read the exam question and write your essay.

> In your English class you have been talking about parents who choose to teach their children at home instead of sending them to school. Your teacher has asked you to write an essay for homework.
>
> Write your essay using all the notes and giving reasons for your point of view.
>
> **Writer 140–190 words.**
>
> **Some children never go to school because their parents teach them at home. Do you think this is a good idea?**
>
> **Notes**
>
> Write about:
> 1  lessons
> 2  making friends
> 3  _____ (your own idea)

4  Ask a friend to read your essay and complete the sentences about it.

I thought the essay was _____ .

The ideas you included were _____ .

The language used was _____ .

You could improve it by _____ .

# CONSOLIDATION

## 🎧 LISTENING

1 🔊 10.04 **Listen to the dialogue between Rob and Carrie. Write the prices of these items and tick the ones that Rob bought.**

1 £_____

3 £_____

2 £_____

4 £_____

2 🔊 10.04 **Listen again and mark the sentences T (true) or F (false).**

1 Rob thinks he's missing £18. ☐

2 He put £10 of credit on his phone. ☐

3 Rob stopped at the ice-cream shop after the bookshop. ☐

4 Carrie suggests that someone could have taken his money. ☐

5 Rob asks Carrie to buy him a cinema ticket. ☐

6 Matt lends Rob £5. ☐

## Ⓖ GRAMMAR

3 **Circle the correct options.**

1 You shouldn't *say / have said* that. She's really upset now.

2 She always travels by bike. She must *be / have been* fit.

3 This time next week I'll *be lying / have been lying* on a beach in Malta.

4 They'll *be / have been* married for 20 years in December.

5 You spent too much. You should *be / have been* more careful with money.

6 No one passed the test. It can't *be / have been* very easy.

7 If it carries on raining like this, we won't *have played / be playing* tennis at three o'clock.

8 This time next year, I will *be studying / have studied* English for four years.

4 **Complete the sentences with two words.**

1 By the time he comes back home, my brother _____ visited 20 countries.

2 This time next week, I'll _____ breakfast in a hotel in Spain.

3 They look very tired. They _____ worked very hard today.

4 You're late! You _____ arrived 30 minutes ago!

5 Someone told me they lost 7–1! They _____ played very well.

## 🅰 VOCABULARY

5 **Match the parts of the sentences.**

1 The crime remains unexplained, ☐

2 Henry hasn't replied to my email, ☐

3 When their team won the match, ☐

4 Several people reported seeing a strange ☐

5 It isn't very valuable. It can't be ☐

6 If you aren't happy, you can bring it ☐

7 There was £25 off this coat in the sale, ☐

8 You've got to buy it. It's only on ☐

a their fans went crazy.

b back to the shop and get a refund.

c so it was a real bargain.

d offer for today.

e and to this day, nobody knows what really happened.

f worth more than £50.

g man running from the crime scene.

h which is really puzzling.

6 **Complete each word.**

1 That's o_ _ – I left my sports bag here five minutes ago and now it's gone.

2 I only paid £3 – it was a real b_ _ _ _ _ _ .

3 There's a r_ _ _ _ _ of £20 for finding the missing cat.

4 I'll tell you but it's a s_ _ _ _ _ and I don't want you to tell anybody.

5 I'm not going to leave the waiter a t_ _ . The service was terrible.

6 Scientists believe the rock is e_ _ _ _ _ _ _ _ _ _ _ _ _ _ _ _ and came from another planet.

7 She definitely works in h_ _ _ _ _ _ _ _ _ . She's either a dentist or a doctor.

8 At only £200, it's really good v_ _ _ _ for money.

## DIALOGUE

7  🔊 10.05  **Complete the dialogue with the phrases in the list. There are two you don't need. Then listen and check.**

> more than likely | you must be joking | a shame
> never mind | same as usual | goes without saying
> don't look at me | how awful

**Milo**  I don't believe it. Someone's spilt coffee all over my project.

**Becky**  ¹_____ . I had nothing to do with it.

**Yildiz**  It was John, ²_____ . He's really clumsy.

**Milo**  Well, it ³_____ that I'm not at all happy about it. It's ruined. Look at it.

**Becky**  ⁴_____ . Can't you do it again?

**Milo**  ⁵_____ . It took me three days and it's got to be handed in tomorrow.

**Yildiz**  That's ⁶_____ . You'll just have to tell the teacher what happened and ask for some more time.

**Milo**  I only hope he'll agree. Just wait until I see John.

## 📖 READING

8  **Read the article and answer the questions.**

1  How did the boys find out how the machine worked?

_____

2  Why didn't anyone at the bank believe their story?

_____

3  What evidence did the boys take back to the bank?

_____

4  What else did they do to show they had hacked into the machine?

_____

5  Why did the bank manager write them a note?

_____

## ✏️ WRITING

9  **Write a paragraph of about 150–200 words on your thoughts about money. Include this information.**

- how you get money
- what you spend it on
- anything you're saving up for
- ways you could get more money

# HONEST TEENS IN CASH MACHINE SCANDAL

When Matthew Hewlett and Caleb Turon decided to try and hack into a cash machine, they could hardly have imagined how easy it would be. The two 14-year-old Canadians had found a manual explaining how to operate the Bank of Montreal ATM online. In the manual there was a password. One day during their lunch break from school they decided to try out the password at the machine in their local supermarket. To their surprise the six-digit password took them straight into the machine's computer, where they were able to access all the data it contained.

The boys went straight to the closest branch of the Bank of Montreal, where they told a cashier what had happened. She immediately told her colleagues, who refused to believe the boys, saying that it was impossible. They said that they couldn't have hacked into the machine and that they had no evidence to support their story. So the boys asked if it would be all right if they got some proof. The bank staff agreed that they could, but told them they would never be able to get anything out of the cash machine.

The boys returned to the machine and hacked it once again. This time they printed out information such as all the cash withdrawals that had been made that day and how much money was in the machine. They also changed the welcome message on the screen to: 'Go away. This machine has been hacked.'

They returned to the bank with the evidence, and this time they were taken seriously. The manager of the bank came to thank them personally. He even wrote them a note to show to their teachers explaining why they were so late back from their lunch break!

# 11 EMERGENCY!

Grammar rap! ▶29

## (G) GRAMMAR
### Verbs followed by gerund or infinitive → SB p.104

1 ★★☆ **Put the words in order to make sentences.**

1 mind / I / you / helping / don't

_____

2 You / buy / can't / it / afford / to

_____

3 promised / tomorrow / to / tell / He / us

_____

4 don't / They / see / their car / expect / again / to

_____

5 She / to / café / suggested / the / going

_____

6 favourite / Imagine / film star / meeting / your

_____

2 ★★☆ **Complete the sentences with the gerund or infinitive form of the verbs in brackets.**

There are some lovely hills near where we live, and we enjoy ¹_____ (walk) there at the weekends. But we have learned ²_____ (be) careful and ³_____ (tell) people where we are going. Usually we avoid ⁴_____ (go) up there if the weather is going to be bad.

But one day we decided ⁵_____ (go) up, even though we'd heard it might get foggy. We really wanted ⁶_____ (get) some exercise. So we set off – the weather was nice and sunny, and everything was great. We didn't expect ⁷_____ (have) any problems.

After two hours, we felt like ⁸_____ (have) a rest, so we sat down. And then the fog started coming in.

My wife suggested ⁹_____ (go) back immediately, but I wanted ¹⁰_____ (stay) a bit longer. Big mistake! Soon we couldn't see anything – we didn't know which way to go at all. My wife called the emergency services. Twenty minutes later, they found us and helped us back home.

I had never imagined ¹¹_____ (need) to make an emergency phone call. And I have promised myself never ¹²_____ (go) into the hills again when the weather forecast isn't good.

3 ★★★ **Complete each sentence with the correct form of a verb from each list.**

> afford | avoid | feel like | miss
> ~~offer~~ | practise | promise

> buy | eat | give | ~~lend~~
> live | speak | study

0 My brother ___*offered to lend*___ me his laptop today so I can do some work.

1 Let's go to the Indian restaurant. I _____ a nice hot curry!

2 Tickets for the concert are really expensive. I can't _____ one.

3 We don't like this city. We really _____ in the country, like we used to.

4 Lily _____ me her answer tomorrow. I hope she says yes.

5 My friends love going to France, because they can _____ French.

6 Jonah always _____ the night before a test.

> ### PRONUNCIATION
> Strong and weak forms: /tuː/ and /tə/
> Go to page 121. 🎧

### to / in order to / so as to → SB p.105

4 ★☆☆ **Choose the correct options.**

Patrick and his friends were really happy because they'd got tickets for the big baseball game. They had queued for three hours the week before ¹*to / not to* get the tickets.

The boys got to the stadium early, ²*so as to / so as not to* have to stand in a long queue. On the way, they stopped at a shop ³*in order to / in order not to* buy some food and drink – they bought a lot ⁴*so as not to / so as to* feel hungry in the middle of the match.

While they were waiting for the match to begin, the sun came out and they took their sweatshirts off ⁵*to / to not* get too hot. And then the game began! Unfortunately, a couple of really big, tall guys sat in front of them, so sometimes the boys had to stand up ⁶*to / not to* see what was happening. But after about an hour, the men left, so for the rest of the game Patrick and his friends had a perfect view.

**5** ⭐⭐☆ **Make the two sentences into one using the words in brackets.**

0 I got up at 6 am. I wanted to get some good photographs. (in order to)
*I got up at 6 am in order to get some good photographs.*

1 The girls got to the lake early. They wanted to get a place in the shade. (so as to)
_____

2 I phoned Michelle. I wanted to invite her to my party. (to)
_____

3 Lachlan didn't tell his parents about the accident. He didn't want to worry them. (so as not to)
_____

4 We took the train. We didn't want to get hot cycling. (in order not to)
_____

5 Mae would like to speak to her. She wants to apologise. (in order to)
_____

6 Are you saving your money? You want to buy a new laptop. (so as to)
_____

## so and such

→ SB p.107

**6** ⭐☆☆ **Circle the correct words.**

1 Samuel was *so* / *such* tired that he just wanted to go to bed.
2 They were *so* / *such* difficult questions that no one could answer them.
3 The water was *so* / *such* cold that we couldn't stay in the pool for more than five minutes!
4 The team drank *so* / *such* much water that we had to get some more.
5 I've lived here *so* / *such* a long time that I can't remember living anywhere else.
6 The concert tickets were *so* / *such* expensive that we couldn't afford them.

**7** ⭐⭐☆ **Complete the gaps with *so* or *such a*.**

1 I need to take an aspirin. I've got _____ bad headache.
2 I was _____ scared that I couldn't move.
3 The food was _____ hot that we had to wait before eating it.
4 Julia told _____ funny joke we couldn't stop laughing.
5 Giorgio was awarded a medal because he had done _____ brave thing.
6 I'm _____ worried about the exam tomorrow.

**8** ⭐⭐⭐ **Read the sentence pairs. Write a new (third) sentence so that it has the same meaning as the sentence pair. Use *so* and *such*.**

0 I'm really hungry. I'm going to eat another sandwich.
*I'm so hungry that I'm going to eat another sandwich.*

1 Maddie's really friendly. I always like being with her.
_____

2 The boys left very early. They were gone before lunch.
_____

3 I've got a bad stomach ache. I might go home.
_____

4 It was a terrible film. We left before the end.
_____

5 The teacher's explanation was complicated. We couldn't understand it.
_____

6 The party was a great success. We're going to have another one next week.
_____

## GET IT RIGHT!

### Verbs with *to* + base form

**With verbs that require *to* + base form, we do not use *for* (+ *to*) + base form.**

✓ I went to the cinema to see a film.
✗ I went to the cinema ~~for to~~ see a film.

**We can use *for* + noun.**

✓ I bought some chocolates for his birthday.
✗ I bought some chocolates ~~for to give~~ him.
✓ I bought some chocolates to give him.

**Tick (✓) the correct sentences. Correct the incorrect ones.**

1 I'm here for English lessons. ☐
_____

2 You need to turn on the light for to see better. ☐
_____

3 He uses his tablet for to read books. ☐
_____

4 I use my phone for taking photos. ☐
_____

5 I asked you to give me information. ☐
_____

6 Giraffes have a long neck for to reach the tops of trees. ☐
_____

 **VOCABULARY**
Danger and safety  SB p.104

**1** ★★☆ **Complete the sentences.**

1 He was very ill, but now the doctors say that he's
o_____ of danger.

2 I can't thank you enough – you s_____ my life!

3 Don't go in there – it's very d_____ .

4 All the passengers s_____ the crash thanks to
the driver's fast thinking.

5 The firefighters found a man in the burning house and
pulled him to s_____ .

6 Their boat sank, but they were r_____
by a passing ship.

7 When we saw the water coming, we knew we were in
d_____ , so we ran to higher ground as fast as
we could.

8 After two weeks in hospital, she finally r_____
and was allowed to go home.

**2** ★★☆ **Complete the story with a word or phrase
in Exercise 1.**

I could see that I was in a very ¹_____ situation.
I was trying to ²_____ the princess's life, but her
enemies were getting very close. Now both of us were
³_____ .

I looked around – how could we escape? There was an
open window, but we were on the fifth floor. I looked
down – we could jump, but I didn't know if we would
⁴_____ the fall. But there were no other options
– jumping was the only way that we could get to
⁵_____ .

I turned to the princess. She looked at me. 'Thank you,'
she said. 'I've been a prisoner here so long. Thank you
for coming to ⁶_____ me.' I smiled. 'No problem,
your Highness,' I said. 'But we're not ⁷_____ yet,
I'm afraid.'

The princess looked out of the window. 'OK,' she
said. 'Let's jump. If we get hurt, there's a chance we'll
⁸_____ before too long.'

I thought: 'How brave she is!' We went to the window.
We held hands and …

'Danny!' said my mum. 'Time for dinner. And stop playing
that computer game!'

## Adjectives with negative prefixes SB p.107

**3** ★☆☆ **Write the negative forms of the words.**

| | | | |
|---|---|---|---|
| 1 happy | _____ | 6 necessary | _____ |
| 2 expensive | _____ | 7 legal | _____ |
| 3 possible | _____ | 8 formal | _____ |
| 4 comfortable | _____ | 9 patient | _____ |
| 5 true | _____ | 10 polite | _____ |

**4** ★★☆ **Complete the sentences with the
words in Exercise 3.**

1 Your little sister's crying – she must be
_____ about something.

2 You don't have to dress smartly – it's an
_____ party.

3 Please don't leave without saying goodbye –
it's_____ .

4 Lunch will be ready in a few minutes –
don't be so _____ !

5 No one can pick up 400 kilograms –
it's _____ !

6 I didn't sleep well – the bed was very
_____ .

7 It's only £5.99 – it's _____ .

8 They didn't need to have all that violence in the
film – it was really _____ .

9 No, I didn't take your backpack – that's
completely _____ !

10 In my country, it's _____
to drive a car if you're under 18.

**5** ★★★ **Complete the conversation with the
words in the list. There are two extra words.**

danger | illegal | impolite | miracle
recovered | rescued | safety | saved
survived | tragedy | trapped
uncomfortable | unhappy | unnecessary

**Arlo** Look, Silvia, I really don't want to be
¹_____ , but can you put your
seat belt on please?

**Silvia** But I hate wearing seat belts, they're very
²_____ . And anyway, I'm in the
back.

**Arlo** I'm sorry, but you have to. It's the law.
It's ³_____ not to wear a seat belt,
even in the back.

**Silvia** Well, to be honest, I think if people drive
carefully, then seat belts are ⁴_____ .

**Arlo** I really don't agree. A friend of mine
was in an accident and her seat belt
⁵_____ her life. She was a passenger
in the back seat of a car that crashed. It's a
⁶_____ that she ⁷_____ .

**Silvia** Really?

**Arlo** Yes, her leg was ⁸_____ . She was
in the car for almost an hour, but the fire
service ⁹_____ her. They took her to
hospital. Her life was in ¹⁰_____ for
almost 24 hours. But she ¹¹_____
OK, I'm happy to say. It was almost a
¹²_____ , though.

**Silvia** OK, you've convinced me. I'm going to
wear a seat belt from now on!

# REFERENCE

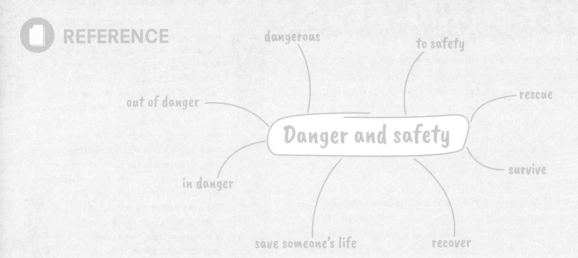

dangerous

to safety

out of danger

rescue

Danger and safety

in danger

survive

save someone's life

recover

## ADJECTIVES WITH NEGATIVE PREFIXES

| il- | im- | in- | ir- | un- |
|---|---|---|---|---|
| illegal<br>illogical | impatient<br>impolite<br>impossible | inexpensive<br>informal | irregular<br>irresponsible | unafraid<br>uncomfortable<br>unconcerned<br>unhappy<br>unhealthy<br>unhelpful<br>unimportant<br>unnecessary<br>unsurprising<br>untrue |

# VOCABULARY EXTRA

1   **Choose a word or phrase from the list that could replace each word in bold.**

> hurt | not dangerous | possibly dangerous
> silly | safe | very frightening

1   Rabbits are **harmless**, so they make good pets.
_____

2   If you concentrate more, you won't make so many **careless** mistakes.
_____

3   Rock climbing is a **risky** sport.
_____

4   The door is locked and windows are closed so the room is **secure**.
_____

5   When Jack fell off his skateboard, he **injured** his arm.
_____

6   The dark cave was **terrifying**. I couldn't wait to get out!
_____

2   **Circle the correct words.**

1   Luckily, we weren't *injured / careless* in the accident.
2   Being out in that storm was a *harmless / terrifying* experience.
3   Make sure the bags are *secure / risky* before you set off.
4   This snake looks dangerous, but it's *harmless / injured* really.
5   I wouldn't ride a bike without a helmet. It's *secure / risky*.
6   Have you lost your phone again? You're so *careless / harmless*!

3   **Complete the sentences with your own ideas.**

1   The most terrifying experience I had was when
_____ .
2   I injured my _____
when _____ .
3   I think _____ (sport) is
risky because _____ .
4   The most secure place to keep valuable things is
_____ .

# THE GREAT *Penguin* RESCUE

In June 2000, a ship called MV Treasure sank near Cape Town, South Africa, causing a massive oil spill. More than a thousand tonnes of oil went into the ocean, near an area where 75,000 penguins lived. Roughly 20,000 African penguins were covered with oil and as a result couldn't swim or even walk properly. It was very unlikely that they would survive, so a huge rescue operation was begun to save them. The operation, which lasted for 12 weeks, was only successful because of the 45,000 volunteers who offered their time and skills for free, in order to rescue the unfortunate birds.

It's an incredible story. At every stage, the rescuers faced enormous problems. First, the penguins had to be caught and transported 800 kilometres by air to a recovery centre. They were then kept in a quiet place for several days so that they could get used to their new home. During this time, and throughout the three months, the penguins had to be fed. As their diet is 98% fish, it isn't easy to find enough fish for 20,000 penguins – they need about ten tonnes a day! What's more, feeding them is dangerous, as they have extremely sharp beaks, and many volunteers got bitten.

Next, the oil had to be removed and to do this, each one of the 20,000 birds was washed by hand. First, the oil had to be removed from their feathers by washing them in detergent and then they had to be dried under special lamps. This was done repeatedly until there was no more oil on their bodies. The penguins then had to be put into pools to swim every day until their feathers had recovered completely.

When the penguins were completely clean and had recovered from their awful experience, they were returned to the wild. They were released into the sea in groups of several hundred at a time. Luckily, penguins are naturally good at finding their way home and it only took them two to three weeks to swim back to the place where they lived.

'The Great Penguin Rescue' was the world's biggest and most successful rescue of live animals. The animal experts and volunteers were the heroes of the rescue. Without them, the penguins would almost certainly not have survived. These people really cared about saving an endangered species.

Dyan deNapoli, who was one of the rescuers, wrote a book about the experience, *The Great Penguin Rescue*. At the time of the oil spill, she was working as a penguin expert at an aquarium in the US. As soon as she heard about the accident, she persuaded her boss to let her go to South Africa to help with the emergency. She knew that the entire species of African penguins was at risk and could become extinct. Her book tells the story of the dramatic rescue and her interest in penguins. The information about this type of seabird, especially African penguins, is interesting and helps readers to understand some of the problems involved in the rescue. Unsurprisingly, the author is now known as the 'Penguin Lady'!

## READING

**1** **What do numbers 1–6 refer to? Match them with letters a–f. Then read the article and check.**

1 1,000+
2 75,000
3 20,000
4 12
5 45,000
6 10

a the number of penguins covered by the oil
b the number of tonnes of fish needed every day to feed the penguins
c the number of tonnes of oil that went into the sea
d the number of weeks that were needed to save the penguins
e the number of penguins that lived in the area
f the number of people who helped to save the penguins

**2** **Read the article again. Answer the questions.**

1 Why was the rescue necessary?
_____

2 Why did the rescue operation work?
_____

3 What were the two problems with feeding the penguins?
_____

4 What made cleaning the penguins so difficult?
_____

5 How did the penguins get back to their original home?
_____

6 Why was Dyan deNapoli so keen to help with the rescue?
_____

**3**  **Read the article again and complete the diagram with facts about penguins.**

1 food
_____

2 body
_____

Penguins

3 abilities
_____

4 status
_____

# DEVELOPING Writing

## A story about a rescue

1 INPUT **Read the story. What lessons did Izzy learn?**

Don't go surfing

1 when you're _____ .

2 when you're _____ .

# RESCUE STORY

① Izzy and her friends had been surfing all day. The others had gone back to the campsite, but she wanted to go into the sea one last time.

② It was so hot that she hadn't worn her wetsuit all day, but now the water felt ¹ <u>cold</u> _____ . She tried to get on her surfboard, but there were such ² <u>strong</u> _____ waves that she was pushed under the water again and again. She soon felt ³ <u>very tired</u> _____ . She started panicking. She tried shouting for help even though she couldn't see anyone nearby.

③ Rory had just got into the sea when he heard Izzy's shouts. As he swam closer, he could see she was in danger. ⁴ <u>Luckily</u> _____ for Izzy, Rory was a firefighter and knew what to do in an emergency. He managed to help her onto her surfboard which he pulled along while he swam to the shore. By this time, the lifeguard had arrived. Rory and the lifeguard thought Izzy was probably suffering from cold water shock, so they wrapped her in dry towels to keep her warm until the ambulance arrived.

④ Izzy soon recovered from her experience, but she now realises how lucky she was that day. Rory had saved her life. If he hadn't reached her so ⁵ <u>fast</u> _____ , she might have drowned.

She understands how ⁶ <u>stupid</u> _____ it was to go into the sea by herself, especially when she was tired because she had been surfing all day. 'I've learned my lesson the hard way,' she says.

2 ANALYSE **Adverbs and extreme adjectives help to make a story more exciting. Replace the <u>underlined</u> words in the story with the adverbs and extreme adjectives in the list.**

> exhausted | fortunately | freezing
> irresponsible | powerful | rapidly

3 **Short sentences can make a story sound more dramatic. <u>Underline</u> the short sentences in the story.**

4 **Match the content (a–d) with the paragraphs (1–4).**

Paragraph 1 ☐     a What happened
Paragraph 2 ☐     b The rescue
Paragraph 3 ☐     c Results/consequences
Paragraph 4 ☐     d Setting the scene

5 PLAN **Choose <u>one</u> of these sentences to begin a story about a rescue. Then make a plan for each of the paragraphs in Exercise 4.**

a The weather was perfect as we set off. What could possibly go wrong?

b It was a bad mistake to go there in the first place.

c 'We were so lucky' is certainly true in this case.

6 PRODUCE **Write your story about a rescue (200–250 words). Use your plan from Exercise 5. Make sure you include all the points in the checklist.**

✓ CHECKLIST

Use some short sentences to add drama to your story.

Include some adjectives and adverbs to make your story exciting.

In the last paragraph, explain how the person felt after the rescue.

 **LISTENING**

1    🔊 11.02   **Listen to the three dialogues. Match what the <u>boy</u> is doing with each dialogue (1–3). There is one extra option.**

a   Saving someone ☐

b   Helping someone ☐

c   Trying to win a competition ☐

d   Giving some news ☐

2    🔊 11.02   **Listen again and mark the sentences T (true) or F (false). Then correct the false sentences.**

1

a   The girl doesn't mind being busy. ☐

b   The boy offers to finish writing the article. ☐

2

a   The boy isn't going out this weekend. ☐

b   The girl decides to go to the music festival. ☐

3

a   A friend of theirs helped to avoid a tragedy. ☐

b   The girl doesn't think Danielle was very brave. ☐

3    🔊 11.02   **Listen again and complete the dialogues.**

1

A   How do you find the time to do so much?

B   I don't know. It just happens. I'm
$^1$_____ I don't know where to start!

A   I just came round $^2$_____ you were free but I don't $^3$_____ you. What can I do?

2

A   How come?

B   $^4$_____ win first prize at the music festival.

A   Well, I'd better buy a ticket for the music festival $^5$_____ miss your winning performance!

3

A   The wind was $^6$_____ he lost control of the boat. He was $^7$_____ crashing into the river bank, but the boat hit a rock instead and he fell into the water.

B   So, you mean Danielle $^8$_____ from the river?

A   Right. She's a strong swimmer and pulled the boy out of the water. Not only that, but she went back in $^9$_____ the boat.

**DIALOGUE**

4   **Put the lines of the dialogues in order.**

1

☐ A   Oh? Why not?

☐ A   Where are you going?

☐ A   Why on earth do you want a new one?

☐ A   To get some things?

☐ B   Into town.

☐ B   To have the same one as everyone else, of course.

☐ B   So as not to spend any money. I'm saving up for a new phone.

☐ B   No, just window shopping today. I'm not going to buy anything.

2

☐ A   A marathon? What on earth for?

☐ A   Why's that?

☐ A   Wow, that's not much food. Not hungry?

☐ A   Fitter? Are you going to start running or something?

☐ B   No, I've just decided I want to eat less.

☐ B   To lose weight and to get fitter.

☐ B   So as to raise money for charity.

☐ B   Actually, I've already started. I go to the gym, too. It's in order to run a marathon.

5   **Write two dialogues of four to six lines each.**

For each one:

•   choose a person from the list below

•   think of 'why' questions to ask the person

•   think of the person's answer(s).

**Look back at Exercise 4 to help you.**

*Someone who wrote a book review*

*Someone who walked 30 kilometres in the snow*

*Someone who wants to be a firefighter*

*Someone who wants to work for a charity*

_____
_____
_____
_____
_____
_____
_____
_____
_____
_____
_____
_____
_____
_____
_____
_____

**READING AND USE OF ENGLISH**
Gapped text

## EXAM GUIDE

**You will read a text from which six sentences have been removed. You have to complete the text by choosing from the sentences in the list. There is one extra sentence which you don't need to use.**

- First, read through the text, ignoring the gaps, for general understanding.
- Pay particular attention to the sentences before and after each gap.
- Think about the type of information needed to fill the gap. Then look at the list of options and choose one.
- Try it in the gap and re-read the paragraph to make sure it makes sense.
- If the gap is the last sentence of a paragraph, read the first sentence of the next one.

1   **You are going to read about a girl who had a scary experience while on holiday. Six sentences have been removed from the text. Choose from the sentences A–G the one that fits each gap (1–6). There is one extra sentence which you do not need to use.**

# Trapped!

Last year Ellie went on holiday to the French Alps with her parents and brother, Ethan. They are all keen mountain climbers and they were looking forward to five days of climbing. They weren't planning to get to any great height, but rather concentrate on a series of challenging smaller climbs.

The first day they tackled a 50-metre cliff face. It was a popular climb and there were several teams doing the same thing. It wasn't too difficult, and they all managed to reach the top within a couple of hours. ¹_____ It was about 11 am and the sun was really starting to warm the rock face. They didn't feel like making the descent in the midday sun, so they decided to wait a few hours and explore the surroundings. Ellie and Ethan set off to investigate some nearby caves. They'd done a bit of caving before and these caves looked pretty exciting. They were deep and dark, but that didn't stop them. After about 10 metres the entrance tunnel became really narrow. Ellie warned her brother they'd better leave. ²_____ He could hear water and was sure there was an underground lake not far ahead. Ellie wasn't so sure, but before she knew it Ethan had squeezed through a narrow gap in the rocks. ³_____ Reluctantly, Ellie started pushing herself through the gap. She was scared. It was pitch black and she couldn't see a thing. She could feel

the cold rock pushing against her chest. She was finding it hard to breathe. And then suddenly she was stuck. ⁴_____ She couldn't move forwards or backwards. She screamed out to Ethan. He could just reach her arm. He grabbed it and pulled and pulled but it was no good. She was going nowhere. Of course, he couldn't go and get help because she was blocking his way out.

For ten minutes they shouted and screamed but no one came. Ellie's body was sore and although the walls of the cave were cold, a hot sweat covered her body. She was beginning to feel dizzy. ⁵_____ The brother and sister began to feel sure they were going to die there.

After what must have been hours, they finally heard voices calling their names. Ellie was too weak to respond, but Ethan called back. Within seconds their parents were with them. Their dad tried pulling Ellie out. When she screamed out in pain, he realised that they needed professional help.

By the time the helicopter arrived more than two hours later, Ellie's body was freezing. ⁶_____ Ellie was hardly conscious when the rescue team finally reached her, but they knew exactly what to do. They sprayed the rock face and then slowly started to pull gently. Then with one last sudden pull, Ellie was free. She'd never felt so happy. Then, amazingly, a few seconds later, she was joined by her brother, who had just squeezed himself back through with no problem at all.

Ellie was taken by helicopter to hospital but released that evening. Apart from a few bad bruises, she was fine.

---

A   Her parents were scared they were going to lose her.

B   He wanted to continue.

C   Ellie's leg was broken in two places.

D   She tried to turn but it was no good.

E   Ethan kept talking to keep her conscious.

F   He called his sister to join him.

G   The views were incredible.

# 12 LIFE'S FIRSTS

Grammar rap!

## GRAMMAR
### Phrasal verbs

→ SB p.112

1 ★☆☆ **Put the words in order to make sentences. For the sentences that contain separable phrasal verbs, write both options.**

1 Rachel / flowers / up / sent / to / cheer / We / her / some

_____

2 quickly / came / after / Louis / operation / round / the

_____

3 away / Maya / looked / our / while / cat / after / we / were

_____

4 excuses / makes / incredible / up / some / Leo

_____

5 couldn't / traffic lights / was / out / so / we / foggy / make / the / It

_____

6 moved / the / coast / Our / neighbours / have / to / away

_____

7 I / sports centre / into / yesterday / Rex / at / ran / the

_____

8 runners / are / many / part / in / the / taking / How / race

_____

9 I / answer / can't / the / out / work

_____

10 the / please / lights / you / on / Can / put

_____

2 ★★☆ **Circle the correct phrasal verb and write it in the correct form. Some verbs are from Unit 7.**

1 You'd better _____ your jacket. It's cold. (put on / take up)

2 I haven't found my travel card yet, but I'm going to _____ looking for it! (carry on / look after)

3 Can you help me? I can't _____ (work out / give up) the meaning of this sentence.

4 I often _____ old friends from primary school when I'm in town. (find out / run into)

5 Paula was really late – she only _____ at ten o'clock. (end up / show up)

6 We've _____ the invitation because we'll be on holiday then. (turn down / put on)

7 My dad has _____ wind surfing. His first lesson was last Monday. (take up / take off)

8 Lily was feeling sad, but we managed to _____ (cheer up / make out) by going for a walk in the park.

3 ★★☆ Circle **the correct options.**

1 We can't *make out / make it out* who the people in this photo are. Do you know?

2 Oh, so you're learning the guitar? When did you *take up it / take it up*?

3 Don't worry about sending me the information. I'll *find it out / find out it* myself.

4 Leroy started learning to dance but *gave up it / gave it up* after a few lessons.

5 My sister isn't well, but my mum's *looking her after / looking after her*.

6 We were going to fly, but when we *worked it out / worked out it*, the train was cheaper.

7 Where's your jacket? You'd better *put it on / put on it* because it's snowing outside!

4 ★★★ **Complete the diary entry with a phrasal verb from the list in the correct form and, where necessary, a pronoun (*it, them, him, her*, etc.).**

| cheer up | end up | find out | give up |
| make up | move away | run into | |
| set off | show up | work out | |

My friend Archie [1]_____ from our town a few months ago and he's feeling a bit down. Last Friday, some friends and I planned a surprise visit to [2]_____ .
We'd [3]_____ an excuse and told Archie to be in the square in his new town at 6 pm.
We [4]_____ straight after school. We missed the first bus because I was late, so we got the next one, but it was the wrong one and we [5]_____ at the bus station! We [6]_____ which bus we needed to catch and finally got to Archie's town at 6.10 pm. We ran to the square, but Archie didn't [7]_____ . Actually, he'd arrived at six, waited for ten minutes and then [8]_____ . We were looking for a café when we [9]_____ Archie along the street! He thought the story of our adventure was really funny – especially when we [10]_____ we'd missed the last bus home! At least our visit was a success: Archie felt happier!

## *I wish / If only* + past perfect   → SB p.115

**5** ★★☆ (Circle) the correct options.

Stefan went to his friend Taylor's party, but he didn't have a very good time. Here's what he thinks.

1 'I wish I *hadn't gone / didn't go* to the party.'

2 'I wish Taylor *hadn't invited / didn't invite* me.'

3 'If only *I knew / I'd known* about the awful music!'

4 'I wish they *accepted / had accepted* the offer of my playlist – but they said it was uncool!'

5 'If only *they'd played / they played* that Katy Perry song – then Kirsty would have danced with me.'

6 'If only Kirsty *had danced / danced* with me! But Freddie was there.'

7 'I wish Freddie *wasn't / hadn't been* there.'

8 'And I wish I *hadn't worn / didn't wear* my yellow trousers and red shirt.'

**6** ★★☆ Read what Kirsty says and write sentences using *I wish* or *If only*.

0 'Stefan didn't ask me to dance.'
   *I wish Stefan had asked me to dance.*

1 'Stefan wore yellow trousers and a red shirt.'
   _____

2 'They played awful music.'
   _____

3 'Freddie wasn't in a good mood.'
   _____

4 'Stefan ate so much food that he felt ill.'
   _____

5 'Freddie laughed at Stefan.'
   _____

6 'Stefan didn't enjoy himself.'
   _____

7 'My parents picked me up at 11 pm. I was the first to leave.'
   _____

8 'I didn't have a good time.'
   _____

**7** ★★★ Look at the pictures. For each person, write a sentence using *I wish* or *if only*.

1 _____
  _____

3 _____
  _____

2 _____
  _____

4 _____
  _____

## GET IT RIGHT!

### Separable verbs

Learners often have problems with word order when using separable verbs.

✓ *I got an invitation, but I turned it down.*

✗ *I got an invitation, but I turned down it.*

**Choose the correct sentence in each pair. Sometimes both sentences are correct.**

1 a I will pick you up at 7.30. ☐
  b I will pick up you at 7.30. ☐

2 a When I left, I forgot to take out my memory stick. ☐
  b When I left, I forgot to take my memory stick out. ☐

3 a I looked for her number on my phone. ☐
  b I looked her number for on my phone. ☐

4 a I tried to solve the puzzle but I couldn't work out it. ☐
  b I tried to solve the puzzle but I couldn't work it out. ☐

5 a I would like to get back my money for that trip. ☐
  b I would like to get my money back for that trip. ☐

6 a You should think over it. ☐
  b You should think it over. ☐

7 a The man gave me my bag back. ☐
  b The man gave me back my bag. ☐

## VOCABULARY
### Phrasal verbs (2)

SB p.112

**1** ★★☆ **Complete the sentences with the correct preposition.**

1 'What's the matter with you?' 'Everything!' 'Cheer _____ . It can't be that bad!'

2 We really missed our neighbours when they moved _____ .

3 They ran _____ some old friends that they hadn't seen for years.

4 How much have we spent today? Let's work it _____ .

5 When the ball hit Matt on the head, he collapsed, but he soon came _____ .

6 I'd put your boots _____ if I were you. It's very wet.

7 They look so like each other – I can never work _____ who is who!

8 Are you taking part _____ the art competition?

9 I can't come out tonight, I'm looking _____ my younger brother.

10 I forgot my glasses. I can't make _____ what's written here.

**2** ★★★ **Complete the dialogues with the correct form of the phrasal verbs in Exercise 1.**

1

A Hey, Lucie. [1]_____ ! What's the matter?

B I'm going to the open day at Manchester University next week, but I'm a bit worried about the journey. I've never been on a train by myself.

A I went there last year. The journey is really easy.

B I've looked at the website but it's really confusing and I can't [2]_____ what I have to do.

A No problem! I'll help you [3]_____ which trains to catch.

B Thanks.

2

A Hey, I [4]_____ Jonathan the other day. Have you heard his family is [5]_____ ? They're going to Cornwall.

B Cornwall? Lucky them! But I'll miss Jonathan. He always [6]_____ in the school swimming competition. I might have a chance of winning now!

3

A Oliver? Could you come straight home?

B Er, OK, mum. Is there a problem?

A I've got to go out in ten minutes and there's no one here to [7]_____ Chloe.

B No problem. I'm [8]_____ my jacket and I'll be back in five minutes.

## Nervousness and fear

SB p.115

**3** ★★☆ **Complete the crossword.**

1 Some people do this if they are very hot or very nervous.

2 If you're frightened, you shouldn't do this. Stay calm.

3 Sometimes people bite these when they are nervous.

4 We often do this when we are very cold or very nervous.

5 extremely scared

6 Some people do this hard when they are tired or afraid.

7 People sometimes do this when they are afraid or nervous.

8 Sometimes this goes dry if you are nervous.

### PRONUNCIATION
Different pronunciations of *ea*
Go to page 121.

**4** ★★★ **Complete the words in the story.**

When I arrived for my interview, I was a bit nervous. They showed me to a waiting room – there were three other people there. One man looked terrible – he was [1]b_____ his n_____ and walking up and down the room. He was walking slowly, but even so, he was [2]b_____ h_____ . The woman was [3]s_____ so much that she had to keep wiping her face. And the other guy looked very scared, [4]t_____ in fact! He was [5]t_____ all the time, and talking to himself very quietly.

I sat down and tried to relax, but it wasn't easy with those people around me. I looked at my hands – they were [6]s_____ a bit, so I took some deep breaths to calm down. 'Don't [7]p_____ ' I said to myself. 'It'll be OK.'

When I finally went in and they asked me a question, my [8]m_____ went completely d_____ and I could hardly speak. I thought the interview had gone really badly. But in the end I got the job!

110

# REFERENCE

to tremble

(your) mouth goes dry

(to be) terrified

to bite your nails

**Nervousness and fear**

to breathe hard

to sweat

to shake

to panic

## PHRASAL VERBS (2)

| | | | | |
|---|---|---|---|---|
| cheer up | look after | make out | put on | take part in |
| come round | make up | move away | run into | work out |

# VOCABULARY *EXTRA*

1 **Match the phrasal verbs (1–5) with the phrases (a–e). Look at the pictures and sentences in Exercise 2 to help you.**

1 break down ☐
2 carry out ☐
3 look into ☐
4 sort out ☐
5 stand out ☐

a do something, e.g. research or experiments
b organise something that is messy or complicated
c a machine stops working
d be different from others in some way
e examine the facts

2 **Complete the sentences with the correct form of the phrasal verbs in Exercise 1.**

1 New cars shouldn't _____ , but ours did!

2 Mum's _____ our holiday. A train trip round Europe!

3 They _____ experiments to find new medicines in this lab.

4 Andy _____ from the other kids in this photo. He looks very smart!

5 The police are _____ the burglary.

3 **Answer the questions with your own ideas.**

1 I'd like scientists to carry out research into _____ .
2 I need to sort out _____ .
3 _____ is a singer/actor who stands out from the others because _____ .
4 I'll never forget the time the _____ broke down because _____ .
5 I think our headteacher needs to look into _____ because _____ .

# IMPORTANT FIRSTS FOR BLACK AMERICANS

In 2008, Barack Obama became the first Black president of the United States. This was another victory in a long history of firsts for people of colour in the US. Here are two more that perhaps you don't know about.

## 1 JACKIE ROBINSON: the first Black player in Major League Baseball (MLB)

Jackie Robinson became an American sporting legend despite a difficult start in life. His family had very little money, but Jackie had plenty of talent and ambition. He was keen on sport from an early age and took up a variety of different sports at school and university. At the age of 26, he decided to concentrate on baseball when he joined his first professional team.

In 1947, Jackie Robinson ran onto the field to play for the Brooklyn Dodgers in New York. Some players, both on the other team and in his own team, weren't happy about playing with him. However, the numbers of Black fans at Dodgers' games started going up. Robinson played baseball exceptionally well, even though he was treated badly for many years by all kinds of people – other players, coaches and fans.

Jackie Robinson was chosen as the best player in the MLB in 1949 and then, in 1962, he became a member of the Baseball Hall of Fame. He was, of course, the first Black player to do so. These weren't his only firsts. He was the first Black baseball reporter on TV and became the first Black vice-president of a major American company.

Jackie Robinson died in 1972, but he is still remembered. In 1992, the MLB announced that no other player would ever wear a number 42 shirt, as that was his number. Since then, the date he took part in his first MLB match has been celebrated as Jackie Robinson Day.

## 2 OPRAH WINFREY: the first Black woman to host a TV show in the US

Oprah Winfrey had a hard life as a child. At the age of six, she moved away from her grandmother and went to live with her mother, but she didn't stay there long because they didn't get on. She ended up with her father, who changed the direction of her life by encouraging her to work hard at school. At the age of 19, while she was still a student, she got her first job in television.

In 1984, Oprah Winfrey became the first Black woman to host a TV show in the US. *The Oprah Winfrey Show*, which ended in 2011, was one of the best-known TV shows in the world. It included interviews with famous people as well as educational features, such as self-improvement ideas and a book club. This was so popular that the books she chose nearly always became bestsellers.

She has appeared in several films, including *The Color Purple*. In April 2000 she launched *O* magazine, which became one of the most successful magazines ever. In 2003, *Forbes* magazine listed her as the first Black woman to become a billionaire. *Time* magazine has included Oprah in their list of the 100 Most Influential People in the World several times.

Although she is one of the highest-paid celebrities ever, she's still busy working on films, television and writing. She also continues to promote education for women and children, and has run national safety campaigns on issues such as encouraging people not to use their phones while driving.

## READING

1  **Read the article and answer the question.**

What was Jackie Robinson's and Oprah Winfrey's life like when they were children?

_____

2  **Read the article again. Mark the sentences T (true) or F (false). Then correct the false sentences.**

1  Jackie Robinson only played basketball at university. ☐

2  Only players on the opposite side didn't want Jackie Robinson to play in Major League Baseball. ☐

3  Many types of people behaved badly towards Robinson. ☐

4  MLB players are proud to wear the number 42 shirt. ☐

5  Oprah Winfrey's father believed education was important. ☐

6  *The Oprah Winfrey Show* was her first job in TV. ☐

7  She works as a teacher for women and children. ☐

3  CRITICAL THINKING **Read the two articles again and find similarities and differences between Jackie Robinson and Oprah Winfrey. Think about their backgrounds, education, careers and achievements.**

A  Similarities:

_____

_____

_____

B  Differences:

_____

_____

_____

# DEVELOPING *Writing*

## A blog entry about a mistake

1  INPUT  **Read the blog entry. What was the result of the writer's mistake?**

_____

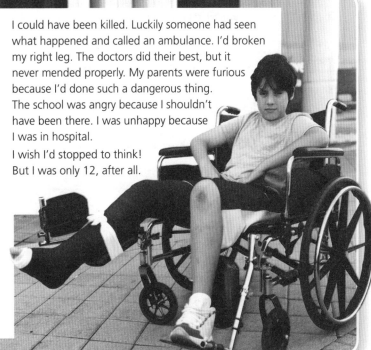

# A BIG mistake

If only I'd stopped to think! That's what I say when I look back at that big mistake. I was 12 and I'd started to play tennis. I couldn't get enough of it. When there was no one to play with, I used to hit tennis balls against a wall. And the best wall was at my school, not far from my house. It was about six metres high. Perfect!

There was a hole in the fence around the school so sometimes I crawled through it, into the school yard to hit tennis balls against that wall. I wasn't supposed to be there after school hours, but I didn't care.

One evening I hit my only ball onto the roof. There it was. Stuck. Now what was I going to do? I had to get it down again. There was a drainpipe on the wall, going up to the roof – I didn't think, I just started to climb. Was I crazy? Absolutely! And what happened? The pipe broke, of course, and I fell.

I could have been killed. Luckily someone had seen what happened and called an ambulance. I'd broken my right leg. The doctors did their best, but it never mended properly. My parents were furious because I'd done such a dangerous thing. The school was angry because I shouldn't have been there. I was unhappy because I was in hospital.

I wish I'd stopped to think! But I was only 12, after all.

2  ANALYSE  Underline **three questions that the writer asks.**

1  Are they really questions for the reader?

_____

2  What effect does the writer want to create by using them?

_____

3  Underline **three single word sentences in the text. Why does the writer do this? Choose the correct answer.**

A  to avoid problems with grammar

B  to create more impact

C  to use fewer words

4  **Rewrite the** underlined **parts. Use either a short question or a single word. There are several possible answers.**

1  I told him the news. This was a mistake!

_____

2  He got really angry and started shouting. I didn't know why he was shouting at me.

_____

3  There was clearly a problem. I didn't know what it was.

_____

4  Then he walked out and closed the door. He closed it loudly.

_____

5  PLAN  **You are going to write a story about a mistake you or someone else made. It can be real or imaginary. Include** one **of these sentences in your story. Then write a plan with your ideas, using the paragraph guide below.**

A  I wish I hadn't said it.

B  If only I'd known that I was breaking the rules.

C  I wish he / she / they had told me.

• First paragraph: Describe the scene / situation

• Middle paragraphs: Tell the story of what happened

• Last paragraph: Explain the result / consequences

6  PRODUCE  **Write your story (200 words). Use your plan from Exercise 5. Make sure you include all the points in the checklist.**

 CHECKLIST

Use an informal style.

Include some one-word sentences.

Ask questions for dramatic effect.

Use phrases that express regret.

## LISTENING

1  ◄)) 12.02  **Listen to two conversations. Answer the questions.**

   1  What does Jamie regret?

   _____

   2  Why is Duncan annoyed with Chiara?

   _____

2  ◄)) 12.02  **Listen again. Answer the questions.**

   1

   a  How much did Jamie pay?

   _____

   b  Why does Anna know so much about buying a smart speaker online?

   _____

   c  What does Anna regret at the end?

   _____

   2

   a  What is the secret that Chiara tells Duncan?

   _____

   b  Why does Chiara think it's OK to tell him the secret?

   _____

   c  Why is it a problem that Chiara has told Sam the secret?

   _____

3  **Complete the dialogues with the correct form of the verbs in the list.**

> do | keep | know | say | tell (x2)

   1

   **Jamie**  No, I didn't know that. But I wish I _____ last week!

   2

   **Jamie**  If only I _____ a bit of research to find out!

   3

   **Anna**  Now I wish I _____ you about it!

   4

   **Chiara**  Did you know his dad had been in prison?

   **Duncan**  No, I didn't, and I wish you _____ me.

   5

   **Chiara**  Well, I wish you _____ something.

   6

   **Duncan**  Sam can't keep a secret and you know it. Oh, if only you _____ quiet!

## DIALOGUE

4  **Put the lines in order to make three short dialogues.**

   1

   **Scott**  Oh Bridget, if only you'd been on time.

   **Bridget**  _____

   **Scott**  _____

   **Bridget**  _____

   **Scott**  _____

   2

   **Raul**  I wish we hadn't come to this restaurant.

   **Frances**  _____

   **Raul**  _____

   **Frances**  _____

   **Raul**  _____

   3

   **Joanne**  My parents are furious with me.

   **Sean**  _____

   **Joanne**  _____

   **Sean**  _____

   **Joanne**  _____

   1  And it's such a shame. The show was amazing.

   2  What? Bad reviews? If only you'd told me that before. We could have gone somewhere else.

   3  I know. But it wasn't my fault. It was the traffic.

   4  I know! If only I'd left when Zac and Sally did – then I wouldn't be in all this trouble.

   5  Yes, exactly. I wish I hadn't gone to that party. I didn't even enjoy it.

   6  But we came here because you said you wanted to eat Indian food.

   7  I wish I had left earlier. But that's history. I missed the show.

   8  I'm not surprised. I found lots of bad reviews online about the food here.

   9  Well, if you didn't enjoy it, why didn't you leave earlier? You're crazy.

   10  There's always traffic. Why didn't you leave home earlier?

   11  Why's that? Is it because you were out late on Saturday?

   12  I know, and usually I love Indian food, but this is awful!

5  **Choose one of the lines below and use it to start or end a five-line dialogue.**

   I wish I hadn't come.

   I wish I'd never bought it.

   If only I hadn't eaten so much.

   If only I'd checked online.

## READING AND USE OF ENGLISH
### Gapped text

1 **You are going to read another extract from *Bullring Kid and Country Cowboy*.
Six sentences have been removed from the text. Choose from the sentences A–G the
one that fits each gap (1–6). There is one extra sentence that you do not need to use.
Look back at the exam guide in Unit 11 on how to answer this question type.**

Fletcher and Fizza climbed quietly down the hill a few more metres and looked out carefully from behind a small bush. Cloudy's kidnapper was talking to another man who he had met on the beach. ¹_____ In the dark they could see that one of them was fat and the other one was thin. It was the thin one that had stolen Cloudy.

'Well done! That looks like a nice horse!' the fat man said.

'Yes, we should get a good price for it,' replied the thin man. 'When's the boat going to get here?'

'Any moment now … I'll get the others,' said the fat man.

He disappeared behind some big rocks in a corner of the beach. After a few seconds, he came back out of the dark. ²_____ 'They're our horses!' whispered Fletcher angrily. 'Those men have been keeping them here!'

The men were obviously waiting for a boat that would get them off the island. A few moments later a green light flashed three times out at sea.

'Hey! That's the sign! They're here!' the thin man shouted.

Fizza and Fletcher realised that if they were going to stop these men, they had to act now before help arrived.

'OK, Fizza,' whispered Fletcher, 'this is what we've got to do …'.

Seconds later, Fizza waited in her position while Fletcher gave a low whistle. All three horses on the sand put their heads up and listened, but the men didn't notice anything. ³_____ Then Fletcher whistled again and the horses began to jump in excitement. This did surprise the men. Every time Fletcher whistled, the horses jumped until they had managed to pull their ropes free from the men's hands. They began to run in circles around them.

'Catch them, stupid!' shouted one of the men.

'You try! They're too quick!' replied the other one.

⁴_____ She ran onto the beach, jumped in the air, gave a high kick and knocked the fat man down to the ground.

'Oi!' shouted the thin man. He tried to run and help his friend, but all three horses moved into his way. ⁵_____ Fizza sat on top of the fat man, who lay face down, and held his arms behind his back.

'Ow! That hurts!' he cried.

'Well, don't move then!' replied Fizza.

She watched as Fletcher tied the thin man's hands and feet together with a rope and then she looked out to sea. ⁶_____ 'What are we going to do when that boat gets here?' she asked Fletcher.

'Yeah!' said the fat man through a mouthful of sand. 'What are you going to do?

---

A He was leading two large horses.

B He couldn't move!

C They were too busy looking for their boat.

D He had three other men with him.

E The lights from the kidnappers' boat were getting much nearer, making the horses run away.

F The men were so close that Fizza and Fletcher could hear them speak.

G This was the moment that Fizza was waiting for.

# CONSOLIDATION

## 🎧 LISTENING

1 🔊 12.03 **Listen to Billy talking about the first time he went surfing. Answer the questions.**

1 How old was he?
_____

2 How long was he in the water for before he went out to the big waves?
_____

3 What did he do when he realised he was alone in the water?
_____

4 Who rescued him?
_____

2 🔊 12.03 **Complete the sentences about Billy with the words in the list. Then listen again and check.**

> confident | embarrassed | excited
> relieved | scared | worried

Billy felt …

1 _____ when his cousins offered to take him surfing.

2 _____ after half an hour in the shallow water.

3 _____ after a few minutes in the deep water.

4 _____ after the big wave hit him.

5 _____ when he saw the lifeguard approaching.

6 _____ when he got back to the beach afterwards.

## 🔤 VOCABULARY

3 **Complete the second sentences with negative prefixes.**

1 It isn't possible.
It's _____ .

2 He isn't very patient.
He's quite _____ .

3 The party isn't formal.
It's an _____ .

4 I expect you to be more responsible.
I don't expect you to be so _____ .

5 This sofa isn't very comfortable.
It's a very _____ .

6 I'm not sure what you're doing is legal.
I think what you're doing is _____ .

4 **Match the parts of the sentences.**

1 The doctors did everything they could to save ☐
2 He's still in hospital, but the doctors say he's out ☐
3 That house is very old. It's in ☐
4 When I get nervous, I can't stop ☐
5 Does your mouth go ☐
6 He got on the wrong train ☐
7 We're moving ☐
8 Come on! Cheer ☐
9 Lena's looking ☐

a danger of falling down.
b and ended up in Glasgow.
c away because Dad's got a new job.
d up. Your marks aren't that bad!
e of danger now.
f after her little sister this afternoon.
g dry when you're scared?
h her life after the accident.
i biting my nails.

## Ⓖ GRAMMAR

5 **Complete the sentences with the correct form of the verbs in brackets.**

1 I haven't got any money for the bus. I wish
I _____ all my money. (not spend)

2 So you don't really enjoy
_____ , you just do it for exercise. (swim)

3 Dad offered _____ us a lift to the party. (give)

4 They've just bought a new car, so they can't afford _____ on holiday this year. (go)

5 If only we _____ more for breakfast. We're really hungry. (eat)

6 We moved to the city last year and I really miss _____ in the countryside. (live)

7 Lisa doesn't mind _____ you. She isn't busy. (help)

8 He wishes he _____ his homework last night. There's no time to do it now. (do)

9 Don't worry about the problem. I'm sure we can _____ . (work out / it)

## DIALOGUE

6   **Put the dialogue in order. Then listen and check.**

| | Assistant | No, no, don't tell me. And keep the keypad covered up with your other hand. |
| | Assistant | Here, let me help you. Put the card in like this and now enter your password. |
| | Assistant | You've got your card in the wrong way. |
| 1 | Assistant | Is this your first time using the cash machine? |
| | Assistant | Well, that's what I'm here for, in order to help our customers. |
| | Assistant | So as to keep it secret. You don't want other people seeing your password. |
| | Man | OK, five, four … |
| | Man | That's so embarrassing. |
| | Man | Of course I don't. You're such a kind young man to help me. |
| | Man | Yes, it is. How did you guess? |
| | Man | Why do I need to do that? |
| | Man | In that case, could you help me with my shopping at the supermarket, too? |

##  READING

7  **Read the article. Circle the correct options.**

### IF YOU DON'T SUCCEED AT FIRST, TRY, TRY AGAIN!

This proverb tells us never to give up on things that go wrong the first time. It must be true because there are plenty of people that carried on trying and ended up famous.

Bill Gates gave up his university course and then started a business which failed. This was before starting Microsoft and inventing Windows – the most popular operating system in the world.

Disney is a global brand today, but Walt Disney didn't have an easy start. Once he lost his job because his boss thought he didn't have any imagination or good ideas! He tried a number of businesses which failed before discovering the secret for success – a little mouse called Mickey.

Who hasn't read *The Cat in the Hat* and the *Harry Potter* series? Well, we might not have had the chance to enjoy them if their authors had listened to all the publishers who refused to print them. Luckily, both Dr Seuss and J. K. Rowling didn't give up until they found publishers that recognised their talents.

Vincent van Gogh, the Dutch artist whose paintings sell for millions of dollars these days, only managed to sell one painting in his lifetime. His lack of success didn't stop him trying though. When he died, he left over 800 completed pictures.

And what about those great scientists? Surely, an intelligent person like Albert Einstein couldn't fail! He was a genius, wasn't he? Well, he was made to leave one school and refused entry to another, but he ended up winning a Nobel Prize for Physics. Then there was Charles Darwin. His father thought he was lazy and uninterested in school. He'd probably be very surprised to find out that Charles' work still influences scientists today.

So, the next time you feel like giving up, stop and think again – you might be a winner one day!

1  The writer *agrees* / *disagrees* with the proverb in the title.
2  Bill Gates *had* / *didn't have* the opportunity to study for a degree.
3  One of Walt Disney's employers suggested that he was *uncreative* / *impolite*.
4  Dr Seuss and J. K. Rowling *offered* / *refused* to sell their books to many publishers.
5  Van Gogh decided to *carry on* / *give up* painting when he couldn't sell many pictures.
6  Einstein and Darwin were both *unsuccessful* / *irresponsible* at school.

## WRITING

8  **Write a short text (150–200 words) about the first time you did something difficult (for example, rode a bike, went swimming in the sea, cooked a meal, or spoke English to a native speaker). Include this information:**

- What it was
- Any problems you had doing it
- How you felt before
- How you felt when it was finished.

# PRONUNCIATION

## UNIT 1
### Linking words with *up*

1 **Match the sentence halves.**

0 I find it difficult to get ___ `d`
1 I've got too much homework. I spend ___
2 Hi, Kelly! What's ___
3 Now that it's winter, why don't you take ___
4 Last night we stayed ___
5 We'd like you to come, but it's ___
6 Have you seen Jim lately? I wonder what he's ___
7 She's ninety now and isn't ___
8 I don't want to move. If it was ___
9 The test has started. Please pick ___

a up? You look really sad!
b up your pen and start writing.
c up to me, I'd stay here.
d up early in the morning.
e up to going for long walks.
f up skiing? It's so much fun!
g up to three hours a night doing it.
h up late talking about our holidays.
i up to these days.
j up to you.

2 🔊 1.01 **Listen, check and repeat.**

3 **Write the phrases with *up* in the column that corresponds to the correct linked sound.**

| | | |
|---|---|---|
| *t* pronounced | _get up_ | _____ |
| *d* pronounced | _____ | _____ |
| *k* pronounced | _____ | _____ |
| *s* pronounced | _____ | _____ |
| *z* pronounced | _____ | _____ |

4 🔊 1.02 **Listen, check and repeat.**

## UNIT 2
### Initial consonant clusters with /s/

1 **Complete the words with the correct letters. These are all /s/ consonant clusters.**

0 I like the top that boy's wearing – the one with black and white _str_ ipes .
1 A ___ong wind was blowing from the east.
2 Her favourite shapes are circles and ___ares.
3 They heard a loud ___ash as the rock fell into the river.
4 She had a headache from looking at the computer ___een all morning.
5 The fire ___ead quickly because of the heat and wind.
6 The people were ___eaming on the roller coaster ride.

2 🔊 2.01 **Listen, check and repeat.**

## UNIT 3
### Strong and weak forms: /ɒv/ and /əv/

1 **Match the questions and answers.**

0 What do you always buy the same brand **of**? ___ `c`
1 What are your favourite shoes made **of**? ___
2 What kinds **of** clothes do you have the most **of**? ___
3 Do you have a lot **of** gadgets? ___
4 Which **of** your gadgets do you use the most? ___

a My mobile phone. Most **of** my friends have one so we text each other a lot.
b They're made **of** leather and they've got rubber soles.
c Chocolate! I love the taste **of** Black & Green.
d I'm quite a casual person. I've got a lot **of** jeans and T-shirts.
e Not really. Most **of** them, like the computer and games console, belong to the whole family.

2 🔊 3.01 **Listen and check.**

3 **Underline** the weak forms (/əv/) and circle the strong forms (/ɒv/) of the word *of* in the sentences.

4 🔊 3.01 **Listen, check and repeat.**

# UNIT 4
## Consonant–vowel word linking

1 **Underline** the words where the final consonant is linked to the vowel sound in the next word.

0 I like that film. It's about two friends who go travelling.

1 I didn't find out who wrote the message.

2 My dad doesn't walk to work anymore.

3 Her family lived in Paris before they came to London.

4 They lost everything when their flat burned down.

5 Jenny's mum gets angry when she doesn't tidy her room.

6 Can we have our break now?

7 It was so difficult to make up my mind!

8 His friends felt awful when Tom told them they'd forgotten his birthday.

9 The climb was difficult, so she gave up before she got to the top.

2 🔊 4.02 **Listen, check and repeat.**

3 **Write the phrases with the linked sound in the correct column.**

| *t* pronounced | *d* pronounced | *k* pronounced | *s* pronounced | *v* pronounced |
|---|---|---|---|---|
| _____ | _____ | _____ | *it's about* | _____ |
| _____ | _____ | _____ | _____ | _____ |

4 🔊 4.03 **Listen, check and repeat.**

# UNIT 5
## The schwa /ə/ in word endings

1 **Complete the words with the correct spelling.**

-ure (x1) | -ent (x2) | -ion (x3) | -ate (x1)
-ous (x3) | -on (x1) | -an (x1) | -al (x3)
-el (x1) | -ul (x1) | -er (x1) | -or (x1)

1 The story will capture your attent____ and imaginat____ .

2 It's a historic____ nov____ about a desper____ and danger____ man.

3 Many fam____ people live in centr____ Lond____ .

4 The hospit____ provided informat____ about the accid____ .

5 They used a pict____ of a beautif____ old wom____ for the advertisem____ .

6 She was the obvi____ choice to direct anoth____ horr____ film.

2 **Although the spelling is different, all of these words end with the same vowel sound. What is it?**

3 🔊 5.02 **Listen, check and repeat.**

# UNIT 6
## The /ʒ/ phoneme

1 🔊 6.01 **Listen and circle the one word in each group which doesn't have the /ʒ/ phoneme.**

| | A | B | C | D |
|---|---|---|---|---|
| 0 | casual | usually | revision | caution |
| 1 | sabotage | version | engine | camouflage |
| 2 | Asia | Russia | treasure | collision |
| 3 | magician | illusionist | occasion | explosion |
| 4 | pleasure | television | pleasant | decision |
| 5 | confusion | revision | measure | permission |
| 6 | unusual | mansion | vision | leisure |
| 7 | exposure | usual | fashion | diversion |
| 8 | erosion | decoration | illusion | invasion |

2 🔊 6.01 **Listen again, check and repeat.**

3 **Complete the sentences with the words in the list.**

Asia | casual | collision | decision | illusionist
occasion | pleasure | revision | usually | version

0 I need to do a lot of ___revision___ because we have a test tomorrow.

1 I don't _____ have to study more than an hour at the weekend.

2 **A** Thank you for helping me today.
**B** It's a _____ .

3 There was a terrible _____ on the motorway today, but no one was hurt.

4 Dynamo is an amazing _____ .

5 I'm saving this beautiful dress to wear for a special _____ .

6 I liked that film, but I prefer the original _____ .

7 I've always wanted to travel around _____ .

8 It wasn't an easy _____ , but I finally chose a career in biology.

9 She prefers _____ clothes and wears jeans and T-shirts most of the time.

4 🔊 6.02 **Listen, check and repeat.**

# UNIT 7
## Intonation – inviting, accepting and refusing invitations

1 🔊 7.02 **Listen to the dialogues. For each one, decide if the speaker is accepting or refusing the invitation and tick the correct box.**

0 Would you like to come with us to see a film on Saturday?
Accepting ☑  Refusing ☐

1 Would you like to work on the History project with me?
Accepting ☐  Refusing ☐

2 Those bags look heavy. Can I help you carry them?
Accepting ☐  Refusing ☐

3 I'm going to ride my bike to the river and go for a swim. Do you want to come?
Accepting ☐  Refusing ☐

4 Didn't you bring anything to eat? Would you like half of my cheese sandwich?
Accepting ☐  Refusing ☐

5 I'm having some friends around for dinner next Saturday. Why don't you join us?
Accepting ☐  Refusing ☐

2 🔊 7.03 **Look at these extracts from the dialogues. For each one, is the speaker accepting (A) or refusing (R) the invitation? Listen to the extracts to check your answers.**

1 I'd love to come! ☐
2 I'm sorry, Pete. ☐
3 That's very kind of you. ☐
4 That's a great idea. ☐
5 Oh, thank you! ☐
6 What a pity! ☐

3 <u>Underline</u> the stressed words in each of the sentences in Exercise 2 and ⭕circle the correct word to complete the rule.

Intonation goes *up / down* when accepting an invitation.
Intonation goes *up / down* when refusing an invitation.

4 🔊 7.03 **Listen, check and repeat.**

# UNIT 8
## Intonation – expressing surprise

1 🔊 8.03 **Read and listen to the dialogue, ignoring the spaces, and answer this question. Why didn't Harriet hold the ladder?**

> ambulance | arm | believe | bookshop
> crash | English | highest | ladder (x2)
> later | mobile | Tell | that | way

**Anna** You're not going to ⁰___*believe*___ this, but…

**Ben** ¹_____ me.

**Anna** Well, Harriet was at the ²_____ yesterday and she asked the shop assistant for the new ³_____ Course Book. It was on the ⁴_____ shelf in the shop!

**Ben** Right.

**Anna** So, the assistant had to get it down using a ⁵_____ . The next thing she knew, he'd fallen and broken his ⁶_____ !

**Ben** No! How did ⁷_____ happen?

**Anna** He asked Harriet to hold the ⁸_____ but she thought he told her to come back ⁹_____ . As she was leaving, she heard this terrible ¹⁰_____ !

**Ben** Really?

**Anna** Yes! At least she had her ¹¹_____ with her. She had to ring for an ¹²_____ !

**Ben** No ¹³_____ !

2 🔊 8.03 **Complete the spaces. Listen again and check.**

3 🔊 8.04 **Ben changes his intonation to express surprise. Listen again, try to notice this, and repeat.**

# UNIT 9
## Moving word stress

1 🔊 9.01 **Listen and mark the stress.**

0 congr•atulate (v)    congratul•ations (n)
1 navigate (v)    navigation (n)
2 mystery (n)    mysterious (adj)
3 artist (n)    artistic (adj)
4 present (v)    present (n)
5 photograph (n)    photography (n)
6 explain (v)    explanation (n)
7 investigate (v)    investigation (n)
8 electric (adj)    electricity (n)
9 music (n)    musician (n)

2 🔊 9.01 **Listen again, check and repeat.**

3  Write the names of the people who do these jobs. Use a dictionary to help you.

0  art                    __artist__
1  music                  _____
2  navigation             _____
3  present (v)            _____
4  investigate            _____
5  electric               _____
6  research (v)           _____

4  🔊 9.02  Listen, check and repeat. Circle the stressed syllable in each of the jobs.

# UNIT 10
## Short and long vowel sounds: /ɪ/ – /iː/ and /ɒ/ – /əʊ/

1  🔊 10.02  Listen and circle the word you hear.

0  ship – sheep        5  not – note
1  sit – seat          6  hop – hope
2  slip – sleep        7  clock – cloak
3  chip – cheap        8  want – won't
4  will – we'll        9  sock – soak

2  Choose one word from each pair in Exercise 1 to complete the sentences.

0  My room's such a mess that I can't find my other ____sock____!
1  Oh my goodness! Look at the _____ – it's time to go home.
2  Now that it's stopped raining, _____ have to go.
3  We're going to the beach and I _____ you can come with us.
4  Her grandparents are _____ farmers.
5  Please _____ down. The doctor will see you in a moment.
6  Danny _____ go to the cinema with us if we decide to see a horror film.
7  I love my new jumper. And it was _____ , too.
8  It's important to get about eight hours' _____ a night.
9  Please make a _____ in your diaries that we don't have a class on Monday.

3  🔊 10.03  Listen, check and repeat.

# UNIT 11
## Strong and weak forms: /tuː/ and /tə/

1  Match the questions and answers.

0  Do you think it's easy **to** make friends when you move **to** a new place?  [d]
1  If it was up **to** you, would you go **to** a hot or cold place for your holiday?  ☐
2  Would you star in a film if you were asked **to**?  ☐
3  Before coming **to** class, who was the last person you spoke **to**?  ☐
4  Which person, living or dead, do you most look up **to**?  ☐
5  What kind of book would you write, if you had **to**?  ☐

a  I'd go **to** the mountains – it would be great **to** go skiing this winter!
b  I talked **to** my mum on my mobile – she wanted **to** know if I was coming home for lunch.
c  Perhaps my grandmother – she's so kind and fun **to** be with.
d  It depends on the place you move **to**. I think it's easier if you go **to** a large town or city.
e  I don't think so – I don't even like going **to** the cinema.
f  Historical fiction, I think. I often think about what it would be like **to** live in the past.

2  🔊 11.01  Listen and check your answers.

3  Underline the weak forms and circle the strong forms of *to* in the sentences in Exercise 1.

4  🔊 11.01  Listen again and check your answers.

# UNIT 12
## Different pronunciations of *ea*

1  Write the words in the correct columns.

bread | break | breakfast | breathe | clean
early | easy | healthy | heard | please
research | speak | steak | sweating | wear

| 1 /iː/ eat | 2 /e/ head | 3 /ɜː/ learn | 4 /eɪ/ great | 5 /eə/ bear |
|------------|------------|--------------|---------------|--------------|
|            | bread      |              |               |              |
|            |            |              |               |              |
|            |            |              |               |              |
|            |            |              |               |              |

2  🔊 12.01  Listen, check and repeat.

# GRAMMAR REFERENCE

## UNIT 1
### Present tenses (review)

To talk about the present, we mostly use the following tenses: present simple, present continuous, present perfect simple and present perfect continuous.

1   We use the present simple to talk about facts and give opinions, and to talk about regular habits.

   It **takes** around four minutes to boil an egg. (fact)
   I **think** this is awful. (opinion)
   I usually **go** to bed around 11 o'clock. (habit)

2   We use the present continuous to talk about what's happening at or around the time of speaking.

   What **are** you **doing**?
   A TV company **is making** a programme about life plans.

3   We use the present perfect simple to talk about past actions and experiences but without saying exactly when. This tense links the present and the past and we often use it when a past event has an effect on the present.

   She'**s read** lots of articles about this and she'**s learned** a lot.
   The storm **has caused** a lot of flooding in the town.

4   We use the present perfect continuous to talk about actions that started in the past and are still happening.

   I'**ve been trying** to get fitter for several weeks now.

### Future tenses (review)

To talk about the future, we mostly use the following tenses: present continuous, *will / won't (do)* and *going to (do)*.

1   We often use the present continuous to talk about future plans and arrangements.

   I'**m having** a guitar lesson tomorrow morning.

2   We often use *will / won't (do)* to make predictions.

   She's very clever – I'm sure she'**ll do** really well at university.
   This is the dry time of year – it **won't rain** again until September.

3   We often use *going to (do)* to talk about intentions.

   Next year, I'**m going to start** university.
   Where **are** you **going to** go on holiday next year?

## UNIT 2
### Narrative tenses (review)

To talk about the past and to tell narratives, we mostly use the following tenses: past simple, past continuous, past perfect simple and past perfect continuous.

1   We use the past simple to talk about actions that happened at one moment in the past, or were true at one time in the past.

   I **fell** over.
   People **didn't have** easy lives two hundred years ago.

2   We use the past continuous to describe ongoing actions or situations around a time in the past.

   I **was running** really fast (and I fell over).
   Thousands of people **were living** in very enclosed spaces.

   We also use the past continuous to talk about an ongoing action that was interrupted by another.

   The fire started while people **were sleeping**.

3   We use the past perfect to describe an event that happened before another.

   The weather **had been** very hot when the fire broke out.
   When we arrived, the film **had** already **started**.

4   We use the past perfect continuous to talk about ongoing actions that began before another action in the past.

   When I finished the race I was exhausted because I'd **been running** for more than two hours.
   He couldn't answer the teacher's question because he **hadn't been listening**.

### *would* and *used to*

1   We use the expression *used to* + verb to talk about habits and customs in the past that are no longer true.

   My mum **used to play football**. (= My mum played football in the past but she doesn't any more.)
   When I was a kid, I **used to listen** to pop music. (= That was my habit but I don't do this any more.)

2   It is also possible to use *would* + verb to talk about habits and customs in the past.

   My dad **would cook** chicken every Sunday. (= This was a custom of my dad's.)
   At school, I **would** always **ask** the teacher questions. (= This was a habit of mine when I was a schoolchild.)

3 The difference between *used to* and *would* is that we can only use *would* for repeated actions – we cannot use it for a permanent state or situation.

*He **used to be** a police officer.* (a permanent state)
*When I was little, I **used to play** in the garden a lot.* (a repeated action)

# UNIT 3
## (don't) have to / ought to / should(n't) / must

1 We use *have to* to say 'this is important or necessary'. We use *must* to say that we, or other people, have an obligation to do something.

*Our train leaves at 7 o'clock, so I **have to get up** early.*
*In our house you **must take** your shoes **off** when you come in.*
*You **must try** to work harder, Jack.*

2 We use *don't have to* to say this is NOT important or necessary.

*You **don't have to come** with us if you don't want to.*

3 We use *should* or *ought to* to tell someone that something is a good idea.

*At the beach you **should put** some sun cream on.*
*That wasn't a nice thing to say – you **ought to say** sorry.*

Remember: *ought to* isn't as frequent as *should*. It is used mostly in writing, and the negative form is rare.

4 We use *shouldn't* to tell someone that something is not a good idea.

*You **shouldn't spend** so much money on clothes.*

## had ('d) / better (not)

We use *had / 'd better (not)* to advise or warn people in strong terms. It is used to tell people about negative results in the future if they do / don't do something.

The form is always past (*had*) and it is often shortened to *'d*.

*You**'d better** hurry up (or you'll miss the train).*
*He**'d better not** say that again (or I will be very angry).*

## can('t) / must(n't)

1 When we want to talk or ask about permission, we often use the modal verb *can / can't*.

*You **can go** to the party but you **can't stay** late.*
***Can** I **borrow** your phone to make a call?*

2 To say what isn't allowed, we use *can't* or *mustn't*.

*You **can't park** here.* (This is a fact / rule.)
*You **mustn't leave** your things on the floor!* (The speaker isn't allowing something.)

# UNIT 4
## First and second conditional (review)

1 We use the first conditional to talk about real situations and their consequences. It consists of two clauses. The *if* + present simple clause introduces the possible situation or condition. The *will / won't* clause gives the result or consequence.

*If you **leave** that door open, the cat **will get** out.*
*If we **don't leave** now, we **won't get** to school on time.*

2 We use the second conditional to talk about hypothetical or very unlikely situations and their (imaginary) consequences. It consists of two clauses. The *if* + past simple clause introduces the hypothetical situation. The *would* clause gives the imagined result or consequence.

*If I **had** a cat, I**'d call** it Max.* (I don't have a cat.)
*If we **didn't have** a cat, we **wouldn't have to** spend money on cat food.* (We have a cat and we need to spend money on cat food.)

## Time conjunctions

We can join ideas about future actions or situations using words such as: *if, unless, until, when, as soon as*.

When we use these words, we use them with the present simple tense (not *will / won't*), even though the clause refers to the future.

*She won't be happy if you **forget** her birthday.*
*We'll be late unless we **leave** now.*
*I won't stop asking you until you **tell** me.*
*They'll be hungry when they **get** here.*
*I'll call you as soon as I **finish** this work.*

## wish and if only

1 We use *wish* or *if only* + past simple to say that we would like a present situation to be different from what it actually is.

*I **wish** I **had** more friends.* (I don't have many friends.)
*My friends **wish** they **were** rich.* (They aren't rich.)

2 We use *wish / if only* + *could* to talk about wanting to have the ability or permission to do something.

*I **wish** I **could** speak Italian.*
*If only you **could** come with me.*

3 If there is a situation we don't like (for example, someone is doing or always does something that annoys us), we can use *wish / if only* + *would(n't)*.

*I **wish** you **would knock** before coming into my room.*
*If only he **wouldn't talk** about football all the time!*

## Third conditional (review)

We use the third conditional to talk about how things might have been different in the past. The third conditional is formed with *If* + past perfect + *would (not) have* + past participle. The third conditional talks about impossible conditions (because the past cannot be changed).

*If I'd been careful, I wouldn't have dropped the camera.*
(I wasn't careful, so I dropped the camera.)
*If you hadn't woken me up, I would have slept for hours.*
(You woke me up so I didn't sleep for hours.)

# UNIT 5
## Relative pronouns

We use relative pronouns to start a relative clause.

1   **To refer to people, we use *who* or *that*.**

*He's a writer. He wrote that fantastic story.*
➜ *He's the writer **who** / **that** wrote that fantastic story.*

2   **To refer to things, we use *which* or *that*.**

*It's a great story. It was made into a film.*
➜ *It's a great story **that** / **which** was made into a film.*

3   **To refer to possessions, we use *whose*.**

*I know a boy. His phone is broken.*
➜ *I know a boy **whose** phone is broken.*

4   **To refer to places, we use *where*.**

*This is the town. I was born here.*
➜ *This is the town **where** I was born.*

## Defining and non-defining relative clauses

There are two kinds of relative clause: <u>defining</u> and <u>non-defining</u>.

1   A defining relative clause identifies an object, a person, a place or a possession. We need this information to know who or what is being talked about. When we write these sentences, we don't use any commas.

*The woman was a genius. She wrote this book.*
➜ *The woman **who wrote this book** was a genius.*
*I saw a film last night. The film was terrible.*
➜ *The film **that I saw last night** was terrible.*

2   We use non-defining relative clauses to add extra information which is not needed to understand the sentence. We put commas around these clauses when we write them. They are rarely used in conversational language.

*My uncle lives in Sydney. He's a very successful writer.* ➜ *My uncle, who lives in Sydney, is a very successful writer.*

## Relative clauses with *which*

1   **When we want to refer back to a whole idea or clause, we use the relative pronoun *which*.**

*He went into the desert alone. It was a dangerous thing to do.*
➜ *He went into the desert alone, **which** was a dangerous thing to do.*

2   **We cannot use *that* or *what* in this way – only *which*.**

*Stephen King has sold millions of books, **which** (~~that~~ / ~~what~~) has made him very rich.*

# UNIT 6
## Present and past passive (review)

1   **We use the passive (present or past) to say what happens or happened to the subject of the sentence. Often the cause of the action is unknown or unimportant.**

2   **We form the passive with a form of the verb *be* and the past participle of the verb.**

*In Canada, English and French **are spoken**.*
*The roof of the house **was destroyed** in the storm.*

3   **We use the preposition *by* to say who or what does the action, but only if this is important.**

*My bike was stolen.* (We don't know, or it isn't important, who stole it.)
*The magic show was watched **by** over 500 people.* (It's important to say who watched the show.)

## *have something done*

1   **We use the structure *have something done* when we talk about someone else doing a function or service for us.**

*My granny's very old, so she has **her meals cooked** for her.* (Another person cooks her meals for her.)
*They **had their car repaired**.* (They paid a mechanic to repair their car.)

2   **It is formed with *have* + noun + past participle.**

*I **had my phone repaired** last week.*

3   **In less formal contexts, *get* often replaces *have*.**

*I'm going to **get my hair done** for the party tonight.*

## Future and present perfect passive (review)

1  **The future passive is formed with *will be / won't be* + past participle.**

   *The new supermarket **will be opened** next week by a famous TV actor.*

2  **The present perfect passive is formed with *have / has (not) been* + past participle.**

   *The streets of our town look awful – they **haven't been cleaned** for two weeks.*

## UNIT 7
### *make / let* and *be allowed to*

1  **We use *make (someone do)* to talk about forcing someone to do something that perhaps they don't want to do.**

   *Our school **makes us wear** a uniform. (= We cannot choose, it's an obligation that our school gives us.)*
   *My sister **made me clean** her bike. (= I could not choose, my sister forced me.)*

2  **We use *let (someone do)* to talk about permission to do the things we want to do.**

   *Our parents **let us sleep** late on Sundays. (= Our parents give us permission to sleep late.)*
   *I **let my brother use** my laptop at the weekend. (= I gave my brother permission to use my laptop.)*

3  **We use *(not) be allowed to (do something)* to say that someone has (or has not) got permission.**

   ***Are* we *allowed to use** our mobile phones in here?*
   *When my parents were children, they **weren't allowed to go** out at night.*

### *be / get used to*

1  **To say that we are (not) accustomed to or (not) comfortable with doing certain things, we can use the expressions *be used to* and *get used to*.**

2  ***Be used to* refers to a state.**

   *She's **not used to eating** dinner so late.*

3  ***Get used to* refers to the change from something we weren't used to, to a situation that we are used to now.**

   *It took her a long time to **get used to wearing** glasses.*

4  **These expressions are followed by a noun or noun phrase, or the gerund (*-ing*) form of a verb.**

   *The animals are not used to **people touching them**.*
   *I'm getting used to **speaking** in public now.*

## UNIT 8
### Reported speech (review)

**We use reported speech to report what someone said in the past. In reported speech, we often have to change the verb that was used in direct speech.**

*'It's 10 o'clock,' she said. ➜ She said it **was** 10 o'clock.*
*'It's **raining**,' my mum said. ➜ My mum said it **was raining**.*
*'I've **had** a really bad day,' he said. ➜ He said he'**d had** a really bad day.*
*'He **didn't remember** to phone me,' I said. ➜ I said he **hadn't remembered** to phone me.*
*'I **can't do** this exercise,' my friend said. ➜ My friend said she **couldn't do** the exercise.*
*'I'**ll pick** you up at eight,' she said. ➜ She said she **would pick** me up at eight.*
*'We'**re going** to tell the police,' she said. ➜ She said they **were going** to tell the police.*

**But sometimes the tense doesn't change.**

*'They'**d stolen** my car,' she said. ➜ She said they'**d stolen** her car.*
*'No one **would** want it to happen,' he said. ➜ He said that no one **would** want it to happen.*

### Reported questions, requests and imperatives

1  **With reported questions, we use statement word order and NOT question word order. We also do not use a question mark.**

   *She asked me **who my friends were**.*
   *(NOT They asked me ~~who were my friends?~~)*
   *I asked her **what she did**.*
   *(NOT I asked her ~~what did she do?~~)*
   *They asked me **why I wanted the job**.*
   *(NOT They asked me ~~why did I want the job?~~)*

2  **When we report yes / no questions, we use *if* (or *whether*) and statement word order.**

   *'Is that book good?'*
   *➜ She asked me **if the book was** good.*
   *'Do you eat fish?'*
   *➜ He asked me **whether I ate fish**.*

3  **When we report *wh-* questions (with *who / where / what / how / when*, etc.), we use the same question word and statement word order.**

   *'What are you looking at?'*
   *➜ He asked me **what I was looking at**.*
   *'Why did you leave the door open?'*
   *➜ They asked me **why I had left the door open**.*
   *'How much money did they steal?'*
   *➜ They asked me **how much money they'd stolen**.*

4  **With requests, we use *asked* + person + *to* (*do*).**

'Please help me with this, Mum.'

➜ He **asked his mum to help** him.

'Can you close the door, please?'

➜ She **asked me to close** the door.

5  **With imperatives, we use *told* + person + (*not*) *to* (*do*).**

'Go away!'

➜ He **told me to go away**.

'Don't phone the police!'

➜ They **told me not to phone** the police.

# UNIT 9
## Modals of deduction (present)

Sometimes we express an opinion about whether something is true or not in the present, based on what we know or can see. We use the modal verbs *must / can't / might / could*.

1  **When we're sure that something is true, we often use *must* + verb.**

They live in a really big house – they **must have** a lot of money.

2  **When we're sure that something isn't true, we often use *can't* + verb.**

That tomato is two weeks old, so it **can't be** good any more.

3  **When we aren't sure, we often use *might* or *could* + verb, to show our uncertainty.**

They're speaking Portuguese, so they **might be** Brazilian.

Perhaps we shouldn't go in there – it **could be** dangerous.

## Modal verbs of deduction (past)

Sometimes we express an opinion about a past situation or event, based on what we know or can see in the present. We use the modal verbs *must / can't / might / could* + *have* + past participle.

The wind blew this tree down. It **must have been** a really strong wind.

The door lock isn't broken, so the thieves **can't have got in** that way.

I'm not sure when my bike was stolen, but it **might have been** yesterday afternoon.

Police think that the criminals **could have taken** more than a million dollars.

## should(n't) have

We use *should / shouldn't have* (*done*) to criticise things that we, or other people, did in the past.

You **should have come** to the party. (= You <u>didn't</u> come to the party, and I think that was a mistake.)

They **should have won**. (= They <u>didn't</u> win, and I think that was bad / wrong.)

You **shouldn't have taken** it without asking me. (= You <u>did</u> take it without asking me, and that was wrong.)

I **shouldn't have said** that. (= I <u>did</u> say it, and I think that I was wrong to do so.)

# UNIT 10
## Future continuous

We use the future continuous to talk about things that will be in progress at a specified time in the future. The future continuous is formed by *will* + *be* + the *-ing* form of the verb.

This time next week, I'**ll be sitting** on a beach in Italy.

Twenty years from now, we **won't be using** money to buy things any more.

## Future perfect

If we want to talk about an action that will have been completed at a specified time in the future, we use the future perfect tense. The future perfect tense is formed by *will* + the present perfect.

Some people think that by 2050, credit cards **will have disappeared**.

By Saturday, I'**ll have spent** all my money – so I won't be able to go out on Sunday.

# UNIT 11
## Verbs followed by gerund or infinitive

Some verbs in English are followed by *to* + infinitive, some are followed by a gerund (the *-ing* form of a verb).

1  **Some common verbs followed by *to* + infinitive are: *afford, choose, decide, expect, hope, learn, offer, promise, want*.**

The show's too expensive – I can't **afford to go**.

The other player's really good, so I don't **expect to win** the match.

You need to **learn to control** yourself and not get so angry.

I **promise to be** there on time.

2   Some common verbs followed by a gerund are: *avoid, enjoy, feel like, finish, imagine, (don't) mind, miss, practise, suggest.*

*That park's a bit dangerous, so we **avoid going** there.*
*I don't want to work any more – I **feel like doing** something to enjoy myself.*
*I can't **imagine living** in a foreign country.*
*Do you ever **miss seeing** your friends when you travel?*

## to / in order to / so as to

1   When we want to give the reason why someone did something (the purpose), we can use *to* + infinitive. We can also use *in order to* or *so as to* – these are more formal.

*I phoned her **to ask** about her about her holiday.*
*It is important to arrive early **in order to save** time.*
*Please fill in this form **so as to help** us provide the best service for you.*

2   When we want to make *in order to* or *so as to* negative, we put *not* before *to*.

*Please speak quietly **in order not to disturb** other users of the library.*
*Please switch off your mobile phones **so as not to spoil** the film for other people.*

## so and such

1   We can use *so* or *such* to emphasise adjectives, adverbs, nouns and noun phrases.

*That's **so expensive**!*
*You walk **so quickly**!*
*He's **such a fool**.*
*It's **such an interesting place** to visit.*

2   We also use *so / such* to show how one thing is the result of another. We use *so* with adjectives and adverbs, and *such (a)* with nouns.

*It was **so expensive** that I couldn't afford to buy it.*
*You walk **so quickly** that I can't keep up with you.*
*He's **such a fool** that I avoid talking to him.*

3   We connect the ideas with the word *that*, but it can be left out.

*The book was so boring (**that**) I didn't finish it.*

# UNIT 12
## Phrasal verbs

A phrasal verb is a combination of a verb with a preposition or an adverb – this creates a new verb which often has a meaning that is completely different from the verb alone. For example, the verb 'look' means 'use your eyes in order to see something', but the phrasal verb 'look after' means 'to take care of someone or something'. Phrasal verbs are very frequent in both spoken and written English.

1   Most phrasal verbs have two parts.

*I can't **work out** the answer. (find by thinking)*
*I always **look after** other people's things. (take care of)*

2   With some phrasal verbs, the two parts can be separated by the object of the verb.

*I **worked out** the answer. OR I **worked** the answer **out**.*

However, when the object is a pronoun, it must come between the two parts.

*I worked it out. (NOT ~~I worked out it.~~)*

3   In other phrasal verbs, these parts can never be separated.

*I **look after** my clothes. (NOT ~~I look my clothes after.~~)*

4   To find out if a phrasal verb can be split or not, look in a dictionary.

If it <u>can</u> be split, it will be listed: work <u>st</u> out.
If it <u>can't</u> be split, it will be listed: look after <u>sb</u>.

5   Some phrasal verbs have more than one meaning.

*My car's **broken down**. (stopped working)*
*When she heard the news, she **broke down**. (started crying).*

## I wish / If only + past perfect

We use *I wish* or *If only* + past perfect to express regret about past actions or events.

*I wish I'd been nice to her. (= I <u>wasn't</u> nice to her, and I am sorry about it.)*
*I wish you hadn't opened it. (= You opened it, and I am sorry about it.)*
*If only I'd listened to my parents. (= I <u>didn't</u> listen to them, and I regret it.)*
*If only we hadn't missed the bus. (= We missed the bus, and I regret it.)*

# IRREGULAR VERBS

| Base form | Past simple | Past participle |
|---|---|---|
| be | was / were | been |
| beat | beat | beaten |
| become | became | become |
| begin | began | begun |
| bite | bit | bitten |
| blow | blew | blown |
| break | broke | broken |
| breed | bred | bred |
| bring | brought | brought |
| build | built | built |
| burn | burned / burnt | burned / burnt |
| buy | bought | bought |
| can | could | – |
| catch | caught | caught |
| choose | chose | chosen |
| come | came | come |
| cost | cost | cost |
| cut | cut | cut |
| do | did | done |
| draw | drew | drawn |
| dream | dreamed / dreamt | dreamed / dreamt |
| drink | drank | drunk |
| drive | drove | driven |
| eat | ate | eaten |
| fall | fell | fallen |
| feel | felt | felt |
| fight | fought | fought |
| find | found | found |
| flee | fled | fled |
| fly | flew | flown |
| forget | forgot | forgotten |
| forgive | forgave | forgiven |
| freeze | froze | frozen |
| get | got | got |
| give | gave | given |
| go | went | gone |
| grow | grew | grown |
| hang | hung | hung |
| have | had | had |
| hear | heard | heard |
| hide | hid | hidden |
| hit | hit | hit |
| hold | held | held |
| hurt | hurt | hurt |
| keep | kept | kept |
| know | knew | known |
| lay | laid | laid |
| lead | led | led |
| learn | learned / learnt | learned / learnt |
| leave | left | left |

| Base form | Past simple | Past participle |
|---|---|---|
| lend | lent | lent |
| let | let | let |
| lie | lay | lain |
| light | lit | lit |
| lose | lost | lost |
| make | made | made |
| mean | meant | meant |
| meet | met | met |
| pay | paid | paid |
| put | put | put |
| quit | quit | quit |
| read | read | read |
| ride | rode | ridden |
| ring | rang | rung |
| rise | rose | risen |
| run | ran | run |
| say | said | said |
| see | saw | seen |
| seek | sought | sought |
| sell | sold | sold |
| send | sent | sent |
| set | set | set |
| shake | shook | shaken |
| shoot | shot | shot |
| show | showed | shown |
| shut | shut | shut |
| sing | sang | sung |
| sink | sank | sunk |
| sit | sat | sat |
| sleep | slept | slept |
| speak | spoke | spoken |
| spend | spent | spent |
| spill | spilled / spilt | spilled / spilt |
| spread | spread | spread |
| stand | stood | stood |
| steal | stole | stolen |
| stick | stuck | stuck |
| strike | struck | struck |
| swim | swam | swum |
| swing | swung | swung |
| take | took | taken |
| teach | taught | taught |
| tell | told | told |
| think | thought | thought |
| throw | threw | thrown |
| understand | understood | understood |
| wake | woke | woken |
| wear | wore | worn |
| win | won | won |
| write | wrote | written |